OLIVER
STONE

OLIVER STONE

Chris Salewicz

ACKNOWLEDGEMENTS

The author would like to express his deepest thanks to Oliver Stone for his great and generous assistance: the amount of time he gave went far beyond the call of duty. James Woods was also sterling in his help. The author would also like to thank the ever-attentive Annie Mei-Ling at Oliver's office, Brian Burden, Jane Hamsher, Don Murphy, Suzanne Fenn, Jonathan Campbell, Perry Henzell, Trevor Dolby, and Julian Alexander.

First published in 1997 by Orion Media
An imprint of Orion Books Ltd
Orion House, 5 Upper St Martin's Lane, London WC2H 9EA

Project editor: Natasha Martyn-Johns
Designed by Leigh Jones

All illustrations supplied by Katz Pictures Ltd.,
The Kobal Collection; Rex Features Ltd.

A CIP catalogue record for this book is available
from the British Library.

ISBN 0 75281 039 1

Colour reproduction by Pixel Colour Ltd., London

Printed in Italy by Printers, Trento

Bound by L.E.G.O., Vicenza

CONTENTS

Introduction

It is early evening. Rays from the dying sun fight their way through the haze of mist that squats over the Pacific Ocean, two blocks to the west. On the top floor of the six-storey Santa Monica office block that houses Illusion Entertainment, the headquarters of Oliver Stone, it is the end of another day.

At the copying machine by the elevators a man in his late twenties photocopies a thick file about Ferdinand Marcos. Dexter King, the film-star-handsome son of Martin Luther King, perches on a desk, making phone calls. In a glass-walled room off the main lobby, deep in conference with several other people, is the former head of the CIA in Laos; he is 'the real thing, like T.E. Lawrence, but without Lawrence's irony – or Peter O'Toole's,' says Stone later.

There is a positive energy that is palpable up here on the sixth floor. The offices, which interlace with loft-style cutting-rooms, are full of young, apparently happy, hard-working people who seem to smile a lot, enjoying the sometimes eccentric foibles and air of moderately amused preoccupation of their mercurial boss.

'Take that down – I want posters of films, not TV series,' he says, motioning jokingly towards an *X Files* poster.

'They have an *X Files* film coming out this summer,' reposts a laughing girl.

'Alright. Then I only want ones that we produce,' he says grinning.

There's a very good atmosphere up here, I tell him. 'Yes,' smiles Oliver Stone enigmatically, 'it's circular.'

Pausing in his progress across the office-space from the cutting-room. Stone stops to inquire mildly of a new employee how she has enjoyed her first day working there.

This is really not how it is meant to be in the kingdom of this supposed *enfant terrible* of modern film: the man who, some say, is the second most powerful creative individual in Hollywood after Steven Spielberg.

Indeed, at the mention of Oliver Stone's name the most rational of people can become irrational. Grown men become nervous or fearful. Vitriol or disdainful groans pour forth from the lips of others.

Yet there is an equal number of loyal adherents to the work of Oliver Stone. In fact, the hostility that he almost automatically provokes is a mark of his success as an *auteur*, and of the colossal confidence signified by his relentless forward course, in which he has taken the subject-matter and moral ethos of the underground press of the late Sixties and massmarketed it via cinema screens. As a consequence, he has created an alternative version of American history, one that resonates deeply with large sections of the community and repels a similarly sizeable quantity. It's all set out in *Platoon*, with its dualistic world of heads and straights, those who get it and those who don't.

Oliver Stone's background is archetypally American in that his background isn't entirely American. There is even a sense of destiny in the manner in which Lou Stone, his Jewish American father, a frustrated writer, sought out Jacqueline Goddet, his French Catholic mother, because he could tell that her 'good French blood' rendered her fine breeding stock.

Born on 15 September 1946, Oliver Stone was raised in Manhattan and Stamford, Connecticut. In what seems to have been an effort at compromise, their son was brought up as a Protestant. With summers spent in France with his relatives (he would write skits that would be performed by his French cousins, the future director charging his family admission), he was given an outsider's view of the United States that perhaps explains the oblique, angular perception he has brought to its political and cultural history and the participants therein.

At first sight Oliver Stone is clearly the antithesis of the bearded, base-ball-capped breed of American film directors who were his Hollywood contemporaries during the second half of the Eighties: with his casual elegance, his lived-in, stubbly face, his dishevelled dark hair and thoughtful speech he has much more the air of a fashionable French media intellectual; but after a moment or two his facial structure – a subtle slant to the eye sockets and high cheek-bones, for example – takes on an angular, Asiatic appearance; it is as though past lives have left an indelible impression, suggesting that his love for the East lies in an ancient part of his soul.

When you question him, Oliver Stone considers every issue with great thought. Sitting in his office, with its photographs of him with Manuel Noriega, Fidel Castro, and Bill Clinton, I ask this most notorious of modern directors what his purpose is in making films. He pauses for a long, long time. Then:

It just came to me that I'm acting out, my need to be. So I'm taking everything I know and putting it into this thing. The sum of my knowledge to some degree is in there. So it's an acting out of my life. What I feel, as opposed to what I don't feel or what I think I feel, what I really feel, what is an authentic feeling. Is it always an interesting illusion? So I think I use it as a mirror, ultimately as a narcissism thing. To look at myself, at my journey through life and how I perceive other people and their struggles. My own experiences in war, and the subject of relationships – marriage, love. So that's a thing that's going on there, perhaps.

There's a dark side to me, always has been. Producers always tell me to lighten up and give some happier endings. And there's some truth in that: that's what *Star Wars* and *Independence Day* are about. Part of me wants to go for it, and part of me resists it: so it's an ongoing acting out. Between having happy endings and sad endings.

Because, [he laughs] I'm not sure how it's going to work out: I'm trying to smile. I have a lot of fun, actually. And I'm having more joy from creativity. Just trying to work on that. You see, I get hammered so much. Some days I'll be subjected to five or six articles attacking me. And you can feel pretty bad about yourself if you let that happen. So I'm trying to let that wash off my back more and more. And just laugh about it – if I can. And just go home and feel good about myself and my real feelings – my real feelings – about myself. And my authenticity, which I believe in. Because it's my experience. And my movies have reflected the way I feel. What I think is authentic.

But I think I've been false, too. I do live falsely sometimes. There's no question of it. But I've lied, I've lied. I've made mistakes. I've lied to myself, rather. There's things that I've not been honest with myself about.

1 Salvador

When *Salvador* sprang on to cinema screens in 1986 it felt like a film you'd been long expecting: assorted unconscious and unrealized anticipations were made manifest by the entrance from out on left field of this major cultural icon. Incontestably, this was a movie of the *zeitgeist*. The arrival of the Beatles, Peckinpah's *The Wild Bunch*, Coppola's *Apocalypse Now*, punk rock...such vastly disparate but equally clean eruptions from the murky swamps brought with them a similarly clear sense that now everything had changed. The fact that this revolutionary film had to struggle for financial success only brought its burgeoning myth an added intensity.

The heightened realism of the plot of *Salvador*, a stinging indictment of US policy in Central America that jumped from high seriousness to absurdity, was served well by its hand-held, low-key documentary style. At a time of *laissez-faire* economics and a thrustingly ambitious yuppie world ruled by Ronald Reagan, *Salvador's* perspective came from the downside, that as experienced by an entire nation sacrificed for the sake of a hedonistic luxury society. The point of the film was driven home even harder by the fact that the service industries of the United States increasingly were manned by immigrants, legal and otherwise, from Latin America.

As a metaphor for the truth behind the American Dream of the mid-Eighties, *Salvador* was beyond compare. It had everything that the yuppie world about it lacked: energy, passion, commitment, vision, as well as a decidedly subjective point of view whose good heart no one could question. And a great story which, as an added bonus, just happened to be based on the truth.

In *Salvador* the 'poetry' of the story often mattered more than the exactness of the facts; as such it provided the template for the future pictures of Oliver Stone, a tone felt in films like *JFK* and *Nixon*, in which compression of characters and facts would be a standard tactic – though no more than it had been for Robert Bolt or William Shakespeare.

'Salvador' is Spanish for 'Saviour', an irony that could hardly be lost on the families of those murdered by the nation's right-wing death squads. However, for Oliver Stone, a maverick outsider who had sought experience and trouble, the film indubitably also did bring personal salvation. To those cosily unaware of the living hell taking place in the tiny Central American country, moreover, it brought a level of at least some understanding.

The making and success of this breakthrough film was, for Oliver Stone, the justification, the validation, of a so far erratic career that had included various periods in the wilderness – some self-created, others a testament to Hollywood's bland, bureaucratic mindset.

After the 1981 flop of *The Hand*, a horror film he made from a screenplay he based on a book by Mark Brandel, his directorial ambitions were blocked. All the same, as a screenwriter with his own distinctive style – the heightened realism of *Salvador* was his stock-in-trade – he had had great success. Most notably, he had won an Academy Award in 1979 for writing the Alan Parker-directed *Midnight Express*. He co-wrote *Conan the Barbarian* with John Milius and *Year of the Dragon* with Michael Cimino; and he had become something of a cult hero, sometimes in dubious quarters, for his *Scarface* script for director Brian De Palma. In the process he had become one of the highest paid scriptwriters in Hollywood.

Armed with a variety of his own heartfelt screenplays, however – there was one called *The Platoon*, another entitled *Born on the Fourth of July* – Stone was desperate to direct again. But all avenues seemed blocked. The film editor Suzanne Fenn, who later would cut *The New Age* for Stone's Ixtlan Productions, remembers running into him from time to time in the Hamptons. 'They won't let me direct, they won't let me direct!' he would complain, grinding his teeth in anguish.

Then one day *Salvador* simply appeared in his life. It was based on the experiences of a photo-journalist called Richard Boyle.

Boyle was a friend of mine off and on. And he was a character. You had to be with him. Chaotic individual. Lives on the edge of his pants. I was hanging out with him here and there. He lived up in San Francisco on a houseboat at the time. He was always fun for a couple of laughs. And we were driving back to the airport and he had a manuscript of short stories and incidents that had occurred in El Salvador. It was oil-stained. He pulled it out of the back seat on the way to the plane. He says, 'You never know: there might be something there.' I read it and I said, 'This is it: this is the greatest story.' I decided to make Boyle the protagonist. And I called him down to LA and I wrote about him. He told me the stories and I put them into screenplay form.

Salvador, the resulting script, was a bloody, black-humoured look at the civil-war-torn Central American country of El Salvador. It was seen through the eyes of a sleazy photo-journalist, a fictional version of Boyle played at peak performance by James Woods, and his drug-addled scumbag sidekick, the DJ Dr Rock (James Belushi). Boyle is eventually redeemed by his love for Maria (Elpedia Carrillo), his Salvadoran girlfriend, whom he smuggles into the United States, only for her to be busted by a border patrol, to be returned to almost certain death in El Salvador. Running as a counterpoint was the subplot of John Cassady, played by John Savage, killed as he fires off revealing shots of the film's dramatic setpiece battle. Boyle at least succeeds in getting his pictures into the USA.

The film included a scene of the killing in his cathedral of Archbishop Romero in 1980, as well as the murder the same year of four American nuns. It also featured a character named Major Max, a composite of several Salvadoran rightists, including Roberto D'Aubuisson, the Arena Party leader who had been accused of complicity in the assassination of Romero: Major Max explicitly orders the death of the archbishop, demanding of a roomful of soldiers, 'Now who will be the one to rid me of this Romero?' – a clear echo of the 'troublesome priest' line about Thomas à Becket used by Robert Bolt, who was something of a mentor to Stone.

Before he had picked up Boyle's scrappy set of stories, Oliver Stone had had little awareness of what was taking place in El Salvador.

> I'd never been. Boyle took me down there and we partied, and went to various ous countries. I didn't know that area, that's why I was stunned to see all that similarity to Vietnam 20 years before.
>
> The kids on the streets were wearing uniforms. America was at war. We were going to go to war then. I think Reagan was planning it. Then the Oliver North situation blew it out of the water and it became a lame duck for the administration when that story broke. Otherwise they would have fought in Nicaragua.

Hoping to film in the country and use its military equipment, Stone had shown the Salvadoran government a version of the script, written by Boyle in Spanish, in which the army wiped out the rebels in battle. For the sake of this deception, he also twisted round the ideology of the death squads, turning their actions into those of the guerrillas.

In March 1985, however, Colonel Ricardo Cienfuegos, the Salvadoran military adviser assigned to the film, was assassinated whilst playing tennis. Then the project was personally turned down by President Duarte, who claimed the film would damage the country's tourist image.

But Hollywood seemed as concerned that the film would damage the image of the United States. *Salvador* was considered actively anti-American by various studios. It followed in the wake of a pair of more conventional Hollywood films about Latin America, Costa-Gavras's Chilean-based *Missing* and *Under Fire*, set during the Sandinista revolution in Nicaragua; both of these had been buried at the box office. Even Stone's initial scheme to minimize the budget by having Boyle and Rock play themselves helped not in the least.

But in the spring of 1985 events took a new turn. The producer Gerald Green, to whom Oliver Stone had given the *Salvador* script, passed it on to John Daly at Hemdale, a British film production company. In the mid-Sixties Daly had formed a management company called Hemdale with the actor David Hemmings. By 1971 they had begun to produce films.

Daly not only loved the script for *Salvador*, but was prepared to finance Stone directing it and its sequel, a film whose title had now been changed to the one word *Platoon*. Oliver Stone could barely believe it:

> I was exhilarated. *Salvador* was the one, and it had been a tremendous struggle. I intended to make a movie by hook or by crook. And John Daly, a delightful kind of British rascal partner, man-in-a-white-suit, Alec Guinness kind of character, made it easier, as did Gerald Green and Arnold Kopelson. They were all really involved. And it was more money than I'd ever dreamed and it got me so I could hire an actor like Jimmy Woods and Jim Belushi, Cynthia Gibb, John Savage, Elpedia Carrillo.... It was a nice little cast that I put together. And I could shoot battles with lots of extras. Barely made it: we ran out of funds in Mexico. It was a rush shoot. Everything went wrong and right and it was wonderful. Very colourful.
>
> What surprised me was when I went back and looked at *Salvador* a couple of years ago: how good it looks. I had the impression that it was this raw documentary-looking movie: it isn't. It's superbly shot. Nicely lit on the whole. Good moving compositions. It's a very technically proficient movie. It seems to me that we all – the director, the DP – had a good sense of what we wanted. I can't believe what it cost. It was a tough shoot.

The 'DP' (Director of Photography) was Robert Richardson, whom Stone would use on all his subsequent films. As he often does, Oliver Stone was going on instinct: Richardson had little feature film experience, except for re-shoot work on Alex Cox's *Repo Man*; he had worked on several documentaries, however, including *Crossfire*, a BBC documentary shot in El Salvador. 'I have only one question for you. Can you cut a long lens with a wide-angle lens?' Oliver Stone demanded of him at their first meeting. When Richardson replied in the affirmative, he got the job.

John Savage (left) and James Woods, as photographer John Cassady and scumbag journalist Richard Boyle in Salvador.

'Bob Richardson is extremely important,' said James Woods. 'He's quiet and he and Oliver are joined at the hip. What he does is the same as Oliver – he grabs stuff you don't expect him to grab.'

Richardson's forte was bold strokes, intermingling plot development and textures in long, sweeping shots. He was also a master at lighting, blending together very classical and very unconventional film lighting: for example, he would pour in a very intense top light which was many stops overexposed, then use a filter so everything would glow.

With El Salvador ruled out, it was decided that the film should be shot in Mexico, with real actors. Locations were set up in the states of Guernero and Morelos and in Mexico City. The budget allowed for 35 days of shooting, for a film which had 93 speaking roles and over a thousand extras. 'I told lies,' Stone told me. 'I said, "This is going to cost three million dollars." And it ended up costing 4.5. For every dollar we had to struggle.'

Originally James Woods had been approached to play Dr Rock, with Martin Sheen pencilled in for Boyle. Woods was so inspired by the part of Boyle, however, that he persuaded Stone he should play him.

He knew of Stone's reputation around Hollywood. 'I'd heard of him as being this crazy, druggy, gifted writer. I liked him right away. His reputation preceded him, bolstered I have to say by Oliver's own efforts: he was very good at getting himself in the headlines of people's minds. But he was never afraid to be who he was.'

Even before they began shooting, Woods began to appreciate that Oliver Stone was a rather different kind of director.

My ex-wife and I were dating after our divorce. Oliver came out to my house, and he said to my ex-wife, 'What kind of clothes do you think Boyle would wear?' She said, 'Oh, I imagined it would be something like a Hawaiian shirt and cowboy boots.' She was an ex-model, that's what she'd been doing. And Oliver suddenly announced, 'Right, you're the costume designer.' She said, 'You're crazy.' He said, 'No I'm not. Here's ten thousand dollars – go down to Mexico City and see what you can do with that.' She's now done some 30 films as costume designer – that's what she does for her living now.

During the making of the film, emotions ran high. On a number of occasions Stone and Woods were even reduced to physically punching each other out; when they ran out of money at one point, Woods even walked off the set. But the film is still the performance of which Woods is most proud. And the one particular scene that he singles out is the one in the cathedral confessional.

Ramon Menendez, the assistant director, is off camera, asking the priest's questions. Woods adlibs the entire one-take scene. 'Have you had carnal knowledge?' Menendez asks him. Woods replies, 'Well yeah, I'm not a saint or anything, but I'm not bad. It's not like I've been out fucking quadrupeds.'

'You had sex with a quadriplegic?' demands Menendez.

'No, with a quadruped, like a goat or a Shetland pony or something.'

After 42 days of shooting in Mexico, the money was finished altogether. Neither the beginning nor the end of the film had yet been shot. Although John Daly at first tried to persuade Stone that those sequences could be dumped, he was eventually cajoled into parting with an additional $300,000. The final week of shooting took place in San Francisco, where the film begins, and in the desert outside Las Vegas.

Then *Salvador* went into the cutting-room. The original running time for the film was two hours 40 minutes.

We were against such odds [remembers Stone]. In the earlier cuts of the film they were fighting me on everything: the rating system... It was just a miracle I got it done. That was a film on which I needed a lot of experience... If I'd been paranoid or irrational or irascible, which I've been accused of, I'd have been buried on that film. It would never have come out. I had so many road-blocks to make that picture. And I got enough of what I wanted in there. I wish there could have been more of me. I did make some cuts for political purposes, to soothe the British distributor, who couldn't get a distribution deal with any American company. Could not! We had to distribute it ourselves. *Salvador* was distributed by Hemdale Leasing Corporation.

In the cutting-room whole scenes were dumped. This was the most famous: while James Belushi gets a blow job under a table, James Woods is having sex with a hooker and at the same time trying to get informa-tion from the drunken colonel; the colonel begins to throw human ears into a champagne glass with the line: 'Left-wing ears, right-wing ears; who gives a fuck? Here's to Salvador.' As he makes a toast, Belushi throws up.

When previewed to US audiences, the comment cards did not show a favourable response to this sequence.

The feeling was that people in America didn't know how they were supposed to react to the movie, [Stone told *Playboy* in 1988], which I found kind of sad. *Dr Strangelove* was a perfect amalgam of humour and seriousness about a subject that is extremely dark. There's no reason the subject of Salvadoran death squads has to be solemn. You can have fun with these guys, 'cause they're assholes.

At the screening in Los Angeles where he first saw the final cut of the film James Woods enjoyed a different response.

> I watched it with the music for the first time. All of a sudden I thought, 'My God: I thought it was this little movie. Am I wrong, or is this a Great Movie?' You don't like to think that a film you're in is a Great Movie: there seems something untoward about it.
>
> Bob Dylan was there and said, 'This is the greatest movie I've ever seen.' People were crying. I thought, 'Jesus, I wonder if we did this?'
>
> *Salvador* [added Woods] is still as cinematically exciting today as it was when it came out, but we've become used to the innovations because they've been used by lesser film-makers. A lot of what he introduced we're now used to. But this was a film that was done for four and a half million dollars in under 50 days.

Something important happened with Salvador: you realized that the problems so many people had had with *Midnight Express*, *Scarface*, and *The Year of the Dragon* were because the films' three directors, Alan Parker, Brian De Palma, and Michael Cimino, prized themselves on being visual stylists; and – though *Scarface* is largely an exception – in their films the feel of Stone's scripts was diluted by gorgeous, tasteful camera moves. When Stone directed his own screenplays he drew out an essence that was gritty and funky, pushing the romance and melodrama to the max in a manner that made for quintessential cinema: *Salvador* was a film of the soul and the heart – as all his later movies would turn out to be – and its immediacy and power were what made you walk out of the cinema unable to speak. No wonder Hollywood hadn't known what to do with him.

2 The Fork in the Road

Its extremely limited release in the United States notwithstanding, *Salvador's* reputation grew unstoppably through word of mouth, greatly assisted by its release on video. By the time the 1987 Academy Awards were announced the film had been nominated for two Oscars; for Best Screenplay and for Best Actor for James Woods' jerky portrayal of Richard Boyle.

When the first reviews appeared, however, Oliver Stone was in the Philippines, shooting *Platoon*.

It was heartbreaking. They told me *Salvador* had opened to no business. And the reviews were mixed to negative. I thought, 'Well, I'm lucky: at least I'm making another movie. I can't dwell on it.' But I was pretty depressed. It came back alive on video. That's where it came into being. I think *Platoon* brought prominence to it and helped it. But John Daly often said – and I think he may be right – that if we'd done *Salvador* after *Platoon* and released it second, it would have been a goldmine. John and I had been, in a friendly way, duelling about the cut on *Salvador*. Yet here he was, going ahead with me on his obligation to *Platoon*. I was amazed. I didn't question it. Don't look the gift horse in the mouth.

Platoon was the film that established Oliver Stone as one of the premiere *auteurs* of the last quarter of the twentieth century. But by the time he came to make it, the film had been in his psyche for so long that he experienced a curious state of distance whilst making it, a sense that perhaps adds to the haunting, dreamlike quality of the final film.

There was a sense of social obligation, of duty. After so many setbacks on *Platoon*...you've no idea. So many times I was said no to that even when they finally said yes in 1986, to be honest I had no exhilaration, no sense of joy. I was totally, 'OK, now I have to go make this picture.'

And I really went about it in a very detached way. It wasn't as though I had a lot of feelings as I was directing it. Nothing like that. I was just sort of dead inside after a while.

Vietnam had been the 'fork in the road' for the young William Oliver Stone.

When he was 15 his parents had divorced, devastating him – he learned that both had been having affairs for years. At this point Stone's stockbroker father revealed to his son that he was heavily in debt. At private school in Pennsylvania he concentrated on his studies, but lived the life of an outsider, a position he maintained when he moved on to Yale. After his first year at Yale, however, he did something that was almost ahead of its time, especially for someone who had considered himself a 'Goldwater Republican': he dropped out.

This turning his back on formal education, however, was done with a plan in mind: his love for the writings of Joseph Conrad had engendered a passion for the East, and he had been accepted for a year's contract at a teaching post at the Pacific Institute in Cholon, the Chinese district of Saigon, the capital of South Vietnam.

> The power of dream in my life was pretty extensive. I followed a dream to Joseph Conrad and I went in that direction in '65 when I went out to Asia. To an Asia that seemed like a dreamland. It was another world, totally at variance with what Joseph Conrad had written. It was a modern Asia that was hard, rich, economically fighting with America, where a war was being fought, Americans were going crazy. It was quite a time – different from Conrad. But anyway, I saw it. And I saw another world, and took a path.

In June 1965 Vietnam was still in the early days of civil war. The American military presence, however, was already sizeable. At this stage the 18-year-old Oliver Stone had no moral qualms about its role what-soever. It was obvious: we're the good guys. He saw Teddy Kennedy on the streets, was thrilled by the presence of the US Marines, and by the sight of the arrival of the First Infantry. There were regular gun battles in the streets of Saigon. With bars that seemed to be permanently open, packed full of gorgeous hookers, it was like living in Dodge City.

> Vietnam was very important [Oliver Stone explained]. Up until then I was living a life where choices were more refined and selected and narrow. I was more of an East Coast/Yale socio-economic clown to that existing generation. I would have gone on, had I stayed at Yale at that time, to be a boy who would have done well I imagine in the corporate structure. I would have emerged as one of the semi-leaders of that world; I would have made a living, married a woman, had the requisite amount of children, perhaps divorced, re-married...I don't know, I'd have been somewhere in that world, and well along now in life. I'd probably have looked the same, even better, and...God knows where I'd be.
>
> But I was never a collegiate type, a country club type. I was never into join-

ing things. I was always an outsider, always alone, always travelled my own path, and I was always regarded with some suspicion by others. It was my nature. I wasn't sure if I was the good guy or the bad guy in the movies. I was the guy they looked at and asked, 'Who the fuck are you?'

The apparently romantic scenario of Vietnam contained all the requisite elements for a young man raised on a diet of Eisenhower-era US foreign policy and the films of John Wayne. It seemed, and he believed, that this was the war of his generation. He became terribly concerned that during his year as a teacher the war would be over and he would miss it.

After two terms Stone quit his teaching job and signed on as a lowly wiper on a US merchant ship, working the South-East Asian ports. After efforts to get a job as a reporter in Saigon, he joined the crew of another US ship, setting sail across the Pacific to Coos Bay, Oregon, in the middle of winter, the ship almost sinking off Alaska.

Back in the States, Stone decided to continue the writing he had started at sea. Moving to Mexico, he rented a cheap hotel room in Guadalajara and in longhand poured out the first four hundred pages of a novel, *A Child's Night Dream*. Influenced by Joyce, J.P. Donleavy, Rimbaud, Norman Mailer, and T.S. Eliot, its central theme was the sorrow of youth, dealing specifically with the idea of teenage suicide, something he had dwelt on after the break-up of his parents' marriage. Thus embarking on a new life, Stone started to call himself by his second name, Oliver, dropping 'Bill', the abbreviated form of William, the name his father had given him.

Back in New York, he moved into his father's apartment; the disapproval of his father notwithstanding, he worked ferociously, defiantly at his novel.

I was bitten by this bug to write this novel. Or rather, that novel had bitten into me – I was like Adam in the garden, it was impossible to ever go back. I could never be a student at Yale after that ever. I could never be part of that system. I was an outsider, a rebel to that. And I knew it.

All the same, heeding the entreaties of his father, he did go back to Yale, in the autumn of 1966. Instead of attending lectures, however, he spent the entire time working on *A Child's Night Dream*, until he was asked to leave. His father was furious, telling him that he would regret this rash decision for the rest of his life. But he was also not without a certain understanding: 'My father – whatever I may say about him – was a very non-pompous individual, who always used to make fun of the professor types at Yale. He prided himself on being more of a common person.'

Back at his father's Manhattan apartment, under his despairing gaze, he completed the book. 'It ends with this weird meditation,' he told me. 'It's this young man writing a suicide note. It's 35 pages of burning, scalding vitriol coming at you.' When it was resoundingly rejected by all the publishers who bothered to read it, the desire to end his life, which had motivated the book, only took a quantum leap; Oliver Stone threw half of the manuscript into New York's East River. *A Child's Night Dream* would finally be published in late 1977.

Then, in April 1967, in what seems almost like an existentialist act, he enlisted as an infantryman in the US Army, asking to be sent to Vietnam. In a twist of fate seemingly loaded with symbolism, he spent his 21st birthday on a plane to Vietnam: this was the day that was lost as his plane journey to fight in Vietnam passed the international date-line, and he thereby missed his legally ordained transference from youth to manhood.

Somebody once wrote that Hell is the impossibility of Reason. That's what this place feels like... I don't even know what I'm doing, a gook could be standing three feet in front of me and I wouldn't know it. I'm so tired... Nobody cares about the new guys, they don't even want to know your name. The unwritten rule is a new guy's life isn't worth as much because he hasn't put his time in... It's better to get it in the first few weeks, the logic being: you don't suffer that much... I think I've made a big mistake coming here.

These words, spoken by Chris Taylor, played by Charlie Sheen, in *Platoon* form the first of the several letters to his grandmother that punctuate the film. To all intents and purposes, Chris was Oliver Stone. 'He was a stand-in. Alter-ego.' Stone would write similar letters to his grandmother, telling her of 'my wishes, my desires'.

It took just one day in the bush for Stone to see through the fallacious romance behind his decision to join the Army. And at the end of the first week in the 25th Infantry he was involved in a night ambush, vividly portrayed in the film: as Stone took the night watch three North Vietnamese Army soldiers walked right up on him. Because they were wearing helmets, his rational brain forced him to believe that they must be lost GIs. Stone froze and was wounded in the neck, probably from a grenade fragment thrown by a fellow American, in the subsequent firefight.

I didn't come from a blue-collar type of background and Vietnam made me very aware of my limitations as a person first of all [Stone told me]. With my own hands and my skin. But it also made me conscious of the six senses: I had to survive. And I became good at it too. I was living on the edges of my body, on the edges of my muscles. I wasn't sleeping for a year. I was out there. I was a

Charlie Sheen, who played Oliver Stone's alter ego Chris Taylor in Platoon.

good soldier too. I smelled like the jungle and I was the jungle. So I fit in.
I was a good soldier – I got a Bronze Star, for combat valour. I did my thing.
But I didn't get carried away. I tried to walk the line.

Wounded a second time, he was sent to a rear echelon unit in Saigon as
a member of the auxiliary military police. After a fight with a sergeant,
however, he cut a deal to be sent back to the field in return for the charges
being dropped. Put in a long-range recon patrol, he met the basis for the
character who became Sergeant Elias in *Platoon*, a part Apache, handsome black-haired man. 'He looked like Jimmy Morrison; he truly was a
Jimmy Morrison of the soldiers. Very charismatic. The leader of the
group. He was killed.'

Moving on to the First Cavalry, he encountered the sergeant who in
Platoon became Elias's shadow, Sergeant Barnes. Stone also won
the Bronze Star for combat gallantry, after charging a foxhole from
which an NVA soldier was pinning down his platoon. What Stone
learned about his own limits and endurance was counterbalanced by
an awakening of consciousness that was very much of its time. Like
that of most other white middle-class Americans, the parameters of
his upbringing had been somewhat limited. For the first time, for
example, he was mixing with blacks and poor whites – his father
was later appalled by the black jive adopted by his son, who during
his time in Vietnam came to love Motown. And his head was particularly opened up by the new music of Acid Rock, by Jimi Hendrix,
Janis Joplin, and Jefferson Airplane, and most especially by the LA
sound of the Doors:

I remember the first time we heard 'Light My Fire': it was a fucking revolution.
In January 1968, I was transferred up to the north. Some of the bunkers – only
about ten per cent of them at this time – had guys in them who'd be smoking
grass and listening to rock – the Doors and Jefferson Airplane, particularly.
These were the heads, and this was the first place I really remember hearing
Jimi Hendrix's guitar playing, which shocked me; I was into classical music
before this.

Like many of his fellow combatants, he discovered the capacity of marijuana for opening his thought processes. 'Getting high as a kite over
there, doing grass. You couldn't handle that shit in combat. You'd do it
in the base camps. Like I did in *Platoon*. I wouldn't walk point like that.
Absolutely not. Furthermore, when shit hits, it also blows away any high
you have, believe me.' On R & R in Australia he continued this internal
journey, with his first LSD experience.

After 360 days in Vietnam, Oliver Stone's time in the Army was over. As
it was for many returning vets, his re-entry into American society was not
easy. Arriving in San Francisco on a Merchant Marine ship with a large
bagful of prime Vietnamese grass, he drifted down the coast to Mexico.
He didn't even bother to tell his parents that he was back.

After a few days in Mexico, he crossed the border back into the States.
His weed supply was now down to two ounces, but he was busted and
found himself on a federal smuggling charge: he faced a possible 25
years in prison. Languishing in the overcrowded San Diego jail with
15,000 other young Americans, he reluctantly called his father. When
his procrastinating court-appointed lawyer was paid a substantial sum
by Lou Stone, he immediately went into action. Oliver Stone's case was
dismissed and expunged from the public record.

Back in New York in 1968, he attempted to make some sense of his
life by writing a screenplay. *Break*, a surreal semi-autobiographical tele-
scoping of various of his experiences with his parents and in Vietnam,
contained the seeds of the Elias and Barnes characters in *Platoon* and
was set to the music of the Doors: Stone even tried to get the script to Jim
Morrison, whom he wanted to play the lead. He heard no more of this
attempt for a long time.

In fact, his Vietnam experiences had led Oliver Stone to appreciate that
film held larger possibilities and fewer restrictions than the written word.

> For me there was a big change in my life when I came back from Vietnam.
> Vietnam was really visceral and I had come from a cerebral existence: study,
> intellectuals, going to school, working with pen and paper, with ideas. I came
> back really visceral. And I think the camera is so much more... That's your inter-
> preter as opposed to a pen. With a pen you can create a one-dimensional char-
> acter. With a camera it's two-dimensional.

Though he was unable to get it off the ground, *Break* was the catalyst that
propelled the 22-year-old Stone to make a decision: to learn this craft
further by attending New York University Film School, on the GI Bill.
Before his course began, he wrote another screenplay, *Dominique: the
Loves of a Woman*. Inspired by Fellini's *Juliet of the Spirits*, the script was
based on the artistic milieu in which his mother lived in New York.

The film school course saved Oliver Stone, especially the teaching of
a young, almost equally manic professor called Martin Scorsese. At one
point, in fact, Oliver Stone felt that he had become like the Travis Bickle
character in Scorsese's subsequent *Taxi Driver*: he was filled with rage
towards Establishment thinking, and even considered killing Nixon
when the President ordered the invasion of Cambodia. But Scorsese
believed in him, encouraging him to make a series of short student films.

All the same, Stone's Vietnam experience led to a sense of distance from many of his fellow students.

People my age didn't understand it. Going to film school was a trip. The kids at the film school were not on the same level, they were not dealing with what I was dealing with. They were into – in my opinion at the time – other kinds of superficial shit: a lot of revolutionary posturing.... I was, frankly, apolitical when I first returned. I was the outsider, just trying to avoid it.

They looked at me a little differently. 'That guy's dark, heavy, so avoid it.' It was kind of like a form of hardness, that's all. I wasn't looking for any sympathy for that. The problem was that a certain portion of this society had fought this war, and others hadn't. So at that point on, we people as a group, veterans, diverged. We'd taken a fork in the road and we didn't realize how severe a fork it was. To return to a society that was, essentially, much more materialistic than the Vietnamese society had been. People were more concerned about money in those days – you forget how big a deal that was.

There was no time for Vietnam veterans. You were a minor subclass. It wasn't a big issue. But a lot of my most radical perceptions certainly appeared in that period: the underclass of American society, what those people had to go through, going to prison... I had a very sharp view of the common man. Still do.

In May 1971 Oliver Stone married Najwa Sarkis, a Lebanese attaché to the Moroccan mission at the United Nations. Ensconced in their new home, Najwa's one-room apartment in Manhattan's East 50s, Oliver Stone wrote his third screenplay, *The Wolves*, the story of the lie at the heart of a Greek dynasty family.

When I was a kid [he said later], I always used to say that I hated New York theatre, because what I knew of it from the edges was very pretentious: people were snooty and they had an attitude that they were better than everybody else. I loved movies better, because not only are they more egalitarian, they were also anonymous: no one knew who the film-makers were then. They were just sort of anonymous: how did they get made? And I loved that anonymity. Which now that I've gone into film I haven't been able to enjoy as much because the world has become so media intense on film-makers that now the film-maker is held to the spotlight. William Wyler didn't have to work that way, I guarantee. Stevens, Zimmerman, Ford – they were all the guys behind the scenes but people didn't really focus on them.

He graduated from film school in September 1971. Immediately he wrote another script, *Once Too Much*, a story with clear autobiographical elements: a college student is busted at the US border with a small amount of marijuana, and the judge gives him the option of going to jail or joining the Marines and serving in Vietnam.

> That whole period from '71 to '76 was a lot of scriptwriting and a lot of doubt as to whether I could really do what I was supposed to do. I'd been exposed to film-making through the film school. But I was working as a taxi-driver and as a messenger, borrowing money from my wife and my father, making ends meet. I was in advertising briefly, trying to get the money from that job just to keep writing. I was working for a sports company and pretending to work on Madison Avenue, but I really hated it and didn't go. A period of doubting whether I would ever do what I really wanted to do, which was to be a dramatist: to make a movie about a subject, write, direct, whatever it took to do all those things. I had a strong vision of what I would like this to be. But I met with much defeat and doubted myself.
>
> Several periods of wilderness in my life. A continuing theme. Exodus 3, Wilderness 2. [Laughs.] Certainly in that early period of my life, the wilderness of not going to Yale, dropping out, what should I do with my life, writing a book that wasn't able to be published – it's very important for you to realize that this was a failure and my father was very tough on me and I didn't admire myself.... And another wilderness after the war and the infantry, a second one. I was in drugs and I went to prison and I was living in the East Village and it didn't look as though I was going to add up to much for my father.

In the unremitting gloom of Oliver Stone's post-film school life, however, there was the occasional ray of light. Inspired by seeing *The Harder They Come*, Perry Henzell's classic Jamaican ghetto tale, Stone travelled down to the Caribbean island to meet the director. 'I smoked a lot of grass. I got stoned in that downtown area, Trenchtown, and I remember they were shooting there that day – gunshots everywhere. I loved *The Harder They Come* and I spent a lot of time with Perry Henzell: they were very sweet to me.'

In 1971 Stone and a friend called Ed Mann had written a screenplay called *Seizure*: it was closely based on a nightmare Stone had had in which he and his wife were living in an old mansion when three maniacs arrived and murdered their guests. Stone had worked as a production assistant on *Sugar Cookies*, a soft-core sex film, and he formed an alliance to make *Seizure* with the two other production assistants, calling the company Euro-American Pictures.

Much of 1972 was spent trying to raise funds until a deal was struck with a Canadian production company: the film was to have the extremely low budget of $150,000. When the Euro-American Pictures team arrived in Canada in 1973, however, they discovered that the production company had gone into bankruptcy. On the spot Stone did a deal with another Canadian producer, in return for which the director gave him virtually all the rights. Eventually, he stole the print and took it over the border into the United States. The film finally got a limited run on New York's 42nd Street in 1974. 'The screenplay includes two or three too many twists but there is some genuinely funny, waspish dialogue,' wrote the *New York Times* reviewer Vincent Canby, who was to become a supporter of the director.

3 Midnight Express

After *Seizure*, Stone began work on another screenplay, *The Cover-up*, loosely based on a suggestion of an imagined government conspiracy behind the Patty Hearst kidnapping. The producer Fernando Ghia passed the script on to Robert Bolt, the esteemed writer of *Lawrence of Arabia*, *Dr Zhivago* and *A Man for All Seasons*. As Stone considered Bolt to be the finest screenwriter in the world, it was an enormous psychological boost when Bolt persuaded Ghia to take out an option on the script, announcing he would work with the writer on a further draft. Not long after the break-up of his marriage, Oliver Stone moved to Los Angeles for a time to work with Bolt.

Although no one was prepared to make *The Cover-up*, Bolt's rigorous approach was both instructive and inspirational for Stone; sufficiently so for him to draw on his inner resources, as well as the characters he had first developed in *Break*, and write the first version of a script that was initially entitled *The Platoon*.

What was more, producer Marty Bregman loved it. But, despite Bregman's best efforts, he couldn't break through the Hollywood wall of apathy about Vietnam. The strength of the writing, however, was recognized. And Columbia's Peter Guber persuaded a somewhat reluctant English director called Alan Parker that here was the ideal writer to adapt a book entitled *Midnight Express* for the film he wanted to make from it.

Midnight Express was written by Billy Hayes, an American tourist who had tried to smuggle 2.2 kilos of hash out of Turkey in 1970 and been busted. He was sentenced to four years, two months in prison. With 53 days left to serve, however, his jail term was arbitrarily extended to 30 years. Not unnaturally he began to plot his escape, and soon afterwards Hayes escaped over the border to freedom in Greece. Subsequently he wrote the book detailing this nightmare; its title came from prisonerspeak for escaping – they would talk in code of 'taking the Midnight Express'.

Although Stone felt that Parker and producer David Puttnam had gone along with Guber's suggestion to use him with some reluctance, he moved to London late in 1977 to work on *Midnight Express*.

> I rented a flat and did the whole bit there. It was winter so it was an indoor
> life and I ended up partying and going out very late until three, four in the
> morning. Getting into English hours, an English thing. Which was fun. It was
> more like Greece, actually. There's something very laid back about England.

Confounding what he believed had been the expectations of Parker and
Puttnam, Oliver Stone turned in a screenplay that grabbed you by the
guts and pressed all available emotional buttons as you were drawn into
Hayes' shocking tale. As a former director of commercials, Alan Parker
was an old hand at manipulating viewers' mindsets and playing with
their most extreme paranoias. And Stone's script for the film tied in
perfectly with this skill. Together they probably put back the Turkish
tourist industry by at least a decade.

Midnight Express graphically exposed the peril of innocents dabbling
in the drug trade in the Third World. As was often the case with Oliver
Stone's early scripts, it offered very much a black and white world,
although with little of the humour and dark irony that pervaded, say, the
later *Salvador* or *Scarface*. In its depiction of the Turks it justifiably drew
charges of racism – although various scenes which would have made
their actions more comic were dropped by the director.

> I think that there was a lack of proportion in the picture regarding the Turks
> [Stone later told *Playboy*]. I was younger. I was more rabid. But I think we
> shouldn't lose sight of what the movie was about. It was about the miscarriage
> of justice, and I think it still comes through. In the original script, there was
> more humour. There were some very funny things that the Turks did, where they
> were portrayed as rather human, too. But Alan Parker does not really have a
> great sense of humour, and I think he moved it in a direction where the humor-
> ous scenes were cut out so that the Turks came out looking tougher, meaner.

While *Midnight Express* was being made in Malta, Stone came across
further subject-matter that he felt expressed the Vietnam experience and
its aftermath in a universal manner. Martin Bregman, who had tried to
get *The Platoon* financed, had optioned *Born on the Fourth of July*, a book
by Ron Kovic, a paraplegic Vietnam veteran who had a burgeoning
reputation as an anti-war activist. Bregman had William Friedkin on
board as director, and Al Pacino was showing great interest in playing the
part of Kovic.

With what seems like an almost poetic prescience, Stone met Kovic for
the first time on 4 July 1978, at a café in Venice, California; among
several people with Kovic was Richard Boyle, a journalist. Kovic was
impressed with Stone and told him he thought he would win an Oscar
one day.

Oliver Stone plunged into writing the screenplay of Kovic's book. His completion of the script, however, coincided with the release of a film with a similar theme: *Coming Home*, starring Jon Voight as a paraplegic vet, with Jane Fonda as his love interest. After the film failed at the box office, Bregnan lost all chance of getting *Born on the Fourth of July* financed. Yet another setback for Oliver Stone with a Vietnam-related film.

Then Stone was approached by Edward R. Pressman, a producer with a similar maverick streak to his own – his family's wealth came from having developed the Mr Potato-head character. Pressman had read the script for *The Platoon* and felt the writer would be perfect for a screenplay based on Robert E. Howard's comic-book hero *Conan the Barbarian*. At one point he even tried to sell the project with Stone inked in as director, but to no avail. Dino de Laurentiis was happy for Stone to write the script, but by the time it was completed, John Milius had been hired as director; to Stone's distress, he rewrote much of his work.

There was some considerable consolation in the offing: when *Midnight Express* was released, in October 1978, the film was immediately a colossal success, both with audiences and critics. And at the 1979 Academy Awards Oliver Stone won the Oscar for Best Adapted Screenplay.

Even this glory, however, was to come to seem like a poisoned chalice. To his contemporaries on the outside, it almost seemed as though Oliver Stone managed to turn the success of *Midnight Express* into prolonged failure.

> I would say the period after *Midnight Express* was tough. I questioned myself again. But then again *Midnight Express* was a miracle in its own way. Because I had a hard time as a screenwriter. I was outspoken in my thoughts in what I wrote. And people wouldn't give me the break. It took me a long time to function in this business. I came out of film school at 23, and until I was 30 I had a hard time. So those seven years were very formative.
>
> Perhaps it was good for me in the long run, because what I'm going through as a film-maker – although I'm known – is in many ways a form of rejection. In many ways it was a form of rejection that that writer went through as well. It built my character. It was tough to keep going when there was so much negativity. It's very difficult to believe in yourself under those conditions. But in fact it was only testing me. There is no end where you finally get accepted. It was just testing me for the same testing that I go through on a daily basis still as a certifiably established film-maker. [Laughs.] There you go. So probably it was just a building of character.

Hollywood – to which he had now moved – played an immediate role in this testing of Oliver Stone: it was utterly resistant, from every angle, to all his efforts to get *The Platoon* made. And now there was an added

Brad Davis as Billy Hayes in Midnight Express**; Oliver Stone won an
Academy Award for a script that did little for the Turkish tourist industry.**

complexity: no longer was this because it was felt there was no audience for Vietnam films; rather, events had overtaken Oliver Stone with the release of two Vietnam films considered epochal, perhaps unsurpassable – Michael Cimino's *The Deer Hunter*, and Francis Ford Coppola's *Apocalypse Now*. Unlike Stone, neither of these directors had served in Vietnam; to add further insult, *Apocalypse Now* had been written by John Milius, with whom Stone had already clashed over *Conan the Barbarian*.

Oliver Stone was beginning to feel deep frustration and anger. His vision was clear. He knew whom he admired as directors: Alfred Hitchcock, Jean Renoir, Jean-Luc Godard, Preston Sturges, John Ford, Stanley Kubrick, Francis Ford Coppola, William Friedkin, Fritz Lang. *Auteurs*, all of them, each with a singular viewpoint and perception. Not unlike himself, in fact. Yet he couldn't get started.

Should he be prepared to take a step back in order to go forward? The lesson of *Seizure*, for example, had not been lost on him. With that film Oliver Stone had learned that horror films are considered to have a ready captive audience and that financing for them is therefore relatively easy to come by. If they would not let him direct what he wanted, then, he figured, he could at least get his foot in the door by returning to the genre.

Accordingly, with Edward Pressman again backing him as producer, he accepted an offer from Orion Pictures to direct *The Hand*, based on *The Lizard's Tail* by Marc Brandel. Brandel's novel told the story of a talented cartoonist who loses his drawing hand in a car crash. As first his career and then his marriage disintegrate, the former cartoonist reveals his true personality. Around him, meanwhile, a series of strange murders take place. Are these being committed by the cartoonist? Or by his severed hand?

In the book the hand is never directly seen. Although Stone's first impulse was to follow suit and never show the hand, he realized that this would not work in cinematic terms. The studio, moreover, seemed to perceive it more in the vein of the shark in *Jaws*. Accordingly, over 30 mechanical hands were produced, at a cost of three-quarters of a million dollars.

All the same, in the perception of Oliver Stone these mechanical hands remained simply manifestations of the anger of Jon Lansdale, the protagonist. 'It's about a man,' Stone told *Mediascene Prevue*, 'and what happens when everything around him begins to break up. His life becomes darker and darker until he explodes – and retaliates.... I renamed it *The Hand*. But that's only a symbol, a symbol of his anger.'

Although Dustin Hoffman, Jon Voight, and Christopher Walken had all been approached to play Jon Lansdale, none of them went for the part. But Michael Caine, who seems never knowingly to have turned down a part offered him, went for it. His consummate professionalism was one of the few positive aspects of making the film: Stone learned from him.

Throughout the shoot the studio was demanding that the film go further and further in the direction of a classic horror film. Stone obliged. But then he cut the film too quickly – and submitted as the studio clumsily exercised its rights of final cut.

Released in April 1981, *The Hand* was not a success, although critically it did not fare too badly. Vincent Canby of the *New York Times* considered it 'a clever horror tale'; Andrew Sarris of the *Village Voice* saw it as 'one of the more intelligent efforts to combine psychological analysis with scary spectacle'.

But other reviewers dumped on the film, as did the box office. *The Hand* had not served its somewhat pragmatic purpose for Oliver Stone. In the larger picture of his career trajectory, however, it would appear to teach him that no compromise was possible whatsoever.

On 7 June 1981 Oliver Stone married Elizabeth Cox, his steady girlfriend and assistant on *The Hand*. For the next five years he worked on a variety of screenplays, including *Defiance*, a script about a dissident in the Soviet Union that he researched there in 1982. It was never made.

But the next project was, and it was one for which Oliver Stone was paid a handsome $300,000. The decision to make a modern version of *Scarface*, based around the almost mythically excessive world of the cocaine trade, was taken after producer Martin Bregman watched the 1932 Howard Hawks film late one night on television.

The tone of the new Oliver Stone version is set at the beginning of the film when Tony Montana, a Cuban 'political prisoner' played by Al Pacino, is interviewed by US immigration officials. 'My father take me to the movies,' he tells them. 'I watch the guys like Humphrey Bogart, James Cagney. I learn how to spe' from those guys. I li'e those guys.'

Oliver Stone modelled his script on *Richard III*, giving it the tone of a comic opera. He researched it in Florida, Colombia, and the Bahamas, interviewing various of the extraordinary participants in a deadly trade that frequently let the streets of Miami run with blood. Tony Montana's story, the product of this research, was that of one of the 25,000 criminals expelled from Cuba among the 125,000 refugees in the boatlift to Miami in May 1980. It tells of his rise and fall in the world of fabulous wealth and egregious violence generated by the cocaine trade. Montana's collapse is made complete by his refusal to heed the cardinal rule of drug-dealing: 'Don't get high on your own supply.' He is also warned never to underestimate the other man's greed.

It was a cathartic screenplay for Oliver Stone. Up until now he had been an increasingly heavy user of cocaine. When the time came to write the script, however, he moved to Paris with Elizabeth his wife and went cold turkey. Perhaps as a consequence, the film shudders with a know-ing resonance. The final sequence, in which Tony Montana buries his face in a mound of cocaine, like a pig wallowing in truffles, must have seemed to Oliver Stone like the way he could have ended up.

Directed with both gusto and skill by Brian De Palma, *Scarface* was released in 1983 to great controversy surrounding its level of violence: an early scene in which a henchman of Tony Montana is dismembered with a chainsaw drew particular attention.

In a positive review of the film, *Newsweek*'s David Ansen got the point about the film's instant reputation as a chamber of horrors. 'De Palma doesn't linger on gore,' he wrote. '...If *Scarface* makes you shudder, it's from what you think you see and from the accumulated tension of this feral landscape.'

Vincent Canby of the *New York Times* also understood the true nature of the film: 'This *Scarface* is too good – too rich in characterizations and too serious in its point of view – to deserve to be classified with the porn movies that glory in their X-iness.'

Many other critics, especially in the United States, were dismissive of the film. Oliver Stone was now earning a Scarface-like reputation for scripts dealing in allegedly gratuitous violence – *New York* magazine's David Denby even referred to him as 'the dread Oliver Stone'.

Scarface did good business in the United States, however. And in Europe, where in many quarters it was hailed as a classic, it did even better. There the sense of spaghetti western-like irony that hung like an aura around Tony Montana was far better appreciated.

The film was a street hit. Its sizeable following and legend has contin-ued on video until the present day: in Mario Van Peebles' 1990 film *New Jack City*, for example, a pivotal scene in the picture's story of a drug baron is played out as *Scarface* is shown on a giant TV screen in the back-ground. Time has served *Scarface* well, both as a piece of work and in terms of its now legendary cult status: in the second half of the 1990s what other films from the same era sell T-shirts containing their protag-onist's image? Why is this? Because Scarface is one of the greatest films of the 1980s, and its subject, like that of the decade, is greed.

To some [Stone told *Playboy*], it's a movie about cars, palaces, money, and coke. It's not just about that. It's about what these things do to you and how they corrupt you. That theme got lost. I think Tony Montana – Al Pacino – has a Frank Sinatra dream of the United States, OK? So he becomes a right-winger in this sense: 'I hate Communists, and this is the good life with the big steaks and the cigars in fancy restaurants and the blonde and the limousines and the whole bit.'

It's the whole group from the Bay of Pigs. A few of them are drug dealers and use drug money to keep their political work going. A lot of these guys have disguised drug dealing as legitimate anti-Castro political activities, and that is mentioned in the movie. Tony's mother tells him, 'Don't give me this bullshit that you're working against Castro, you know. I know you. You've always been a gangster and you're going to die one.'

As with *Midnight Express*, some of the criticism aimed at *Scarface* concerned the negative image it gave to a minority ethnic group. For his next screenplay, Oliver Stone was to meet with even greater animosity as similar charges were again levelled at him.

Year of the Dragon was the comeback film for *Deerhunter* director Michael Cimino; after being lauded as one of Hollywood's brightest young hopes for his multiple-Oscar-winning film, Cimino had been vilified and virtually run out of town for the supposed disaster of *Heaven's Gate*. Who better for him to work with on a screenplay than Oliver Stone, who by now was also attracting endless controversy?

Like *Midnight Express*, *Year of the Dragon* was adapted from a novel, Robert Daley's 1981 book of the same name. Set in Manhattan's Chinatown, it concerned the efforts of Stanley White (Mickey Rourke), a much decorated New York detective and Vietnam veteran, to almost singlehandedly destroy heroin trafficking by Chinese Triads. There are scenes of spectacular action worthy of John Woo, most notably a gun battle in a crowded Chinese restaurant. White's estranged wife (Caroline Kava) is murdered on the orders of the ambitious Joey Tai, played strikingly by John Lone, and his new girlfriend, a beautiful Chinese TV reporter (Ariane), is gang-raped. In a final Western-like showdown on some dockside railway tracks, White and Tai run at each other firing their weapons until the Chinese crime boss is wounded: White permits him to commit suicide. The Western shoot-out ending was archetypal – fittingly, for White's entire ethos is that of a lone sheriff attempting to clean up the town.

So yet again Oliver Stone was accused of racism, this time for depicting members of the Chinese community as being involved in an international conspiracy to dominate the world heroin trade. Yet what Stone posited was the truth: the heroin boom of the early Eighties was due to expansionist moves by Chinese heroin warlords – often former generals in the defeated Chiang Kai-Shek's Chinese national army – operating in the border country between Thailand and Burma: there are scenes in Thailand to this effect in *Year of the Dragon*.

This was one of Mickey Rourke's first major parts, a leap of faith for Cimino. The fact that his character was a second-generation Polish American who had returned from a tour of duty in Vietnam filled with bile towards Asians in general also caused consternation. Why should a member of one minority group be hostile towards members of another?

Yet this is exactly what happens the world over. Indeed, it is through White's love for his Chinese girlfriend that his anger at Asians is resolved.

Aware that Michael Cimino and Oliver Stone had been very much a double act in the creation of this film, Pauline Kael launched a vicious attack on them, writing that 'in terms of controlling moral intelligence Oliver Stone and Michael Cimino are still living in a cave... One brazen vulgarian working on a movie might enliven it, but two – and both xeno-phobic – bring out the worst in each other.' Clearly, Pauline Kael did not appreciate the movie's finer points. Nor did the *Village Voice*'s Andrew Sarris. '*Dragon* is a thoroughly rotten movie,' he wrote.

Three years later, in the *Playboy* interview, Stone responded to some of the criticisms of *Year of the Dragon*:

> The Chinese want to believe that there are no gangsters among them. That's all horseshit! The Chinese are the greatest importers of heroin in this country. We knew this five years ago! As for the lead character, played by Mickey Rourke, he is a racist and we wrote him that way...but I think people cheered him for other reasons, not for his racism. At least I hope not. But there might be an element of it. The guy, no matter how prejudiced, is still trying to get some-thing done – as an underdog. That's why I'm rooting for him. But I should say that I think it was the least successful of my scripts.

Oliver Stone had had an ulterior motive for writing *Year of the Dragon*. He had accepted 'only' $200,000 in exchange for a promise by Dino de Laurentiis, the film's producer, that he would then produce *Platoon*. The project seemed to have a green light: Stone cast it and scouted locations in the Philippines.

De Laurentiis, however, ran into stumbling blocks: although he had ready the $5 to $6 million for making the film, he couldn't find a distrib-utor to go in with him. Oliver Stone was devastated when he heard that the producer had decided he felt he could no longer go ahead. But his despair was only to grow: de Laurentiis maintained that because of the money he had laid out for Stone's trip to the Philippines, he would keep control of the *Platoon* script until the money was repaid.

This was not the only problem Oliver Stone was having with a script. After having written *Eight Million Ways to Die* for director Hal Ashby, Stone learned that Ashby had had it substantially rewritten by renowned 'script doctor' Robert Towne. The setting of the film had been shifted from New York to Los Angeles. When Oliver Stone visited the Malibu set of the film, he found it a textbook example of movie-making excess: if he ever got to direct again, he vowed, it would never be in such a manner.

All the same life continued: on 29 December 1984, Oliver Stone's wife Elizabeth gave birth to their first child, a boy, whom they called Sean Christopher. But the following March Oliver Stone's father died, aged 75. Before he passed on, the differences between the father and son were resolved: there will always be a need for good stories, Lou Stone told Oliver.

There were other changes under way. By now Oliver Stone had gone down to Central America with Richard Boyle, the journalist whom he had met with Ron Kovic, and was working on the script for *Salvador*. John Daly was about to come into Oliver Stone's life. *Salvador* would be made, followed by *Platoon*. The years of quiet hell were almost over.

4 Platoon

'Rejoice, O young man, in thy youth' – Ecclesiastes.

The autobiographical *Platoon* is hinged around four combat missions. Each reflects the growing experience of Chris Taylor, the protagonist. Cast as an innocent into a world of good and evil, he comes to find himself through the conflict of battle, both against the North Vietnamese and the enemy within, at base camp. But isn't he crazy to be there at all? Certainly that is what his fellow soldiers think. As he pulls the outhouse barrels with the black King, he describes how he 'dropped out of college and told 'em I wanted infantry, combat, and Nam'.

'Sheeit, gotta be rich in the first place to think like that,' exclaims King. And perhaps there had been some truth in that for Oliver Stone.

Platoon is set in a world of black and white, good and evil. It is a grunt's tale. Apart from the responses of the terrified villagers we learn little or nothing about the feelings of the Vietnamese. But the commentary comes from within the plot, between those of higher consciousness and those of lower. And the conflicts create a world that is extraordinarily moving. It was, as Vincent Canby wrote in his *New York Times* review, 'as full of passion as it is of redeeming scary irony'.

By examining the various lives and attitudes of the members of the platoon, we come to learn why America was in Vietnam. The film was the complete antithesis of the cod patriotism espoused in such ultimate Reagan era films as *Top Gun* and the *Rambo* series. Hammering the point home a little too knowingly, the good guys, who are mostly black, smoke Kools, the bad guys Marlboros. 'It's not a Vietnam movie, it's a thriller set in the jungle,' was how Oliver Stone had described his concept of the film to *Mediascene Prevue* six years before. 'It's like *Summer of '42*, except in the jungle. The lead character goes in as a kid, meets a series of people unlike any he's ever met before in his life. They train him, they raise him. Mowgli, the jungle boy....'

Filming began in February 1986. Stone had mustered a sterling cast. Although James Woods had turned him down ('I couldn't face going into another jungle with Oliver'), rising 'Brat Pack' star Charlie Sheen was chosen for the lead role of Chris Taylor. Tom Berenger and Willem Dafoe, meanwhile, were set to play opposite each other as the dark Barnes, his face grotesquely scarred, like a parody of a Prussian duelling scar, and the light Elias. In the scene in the jungle in which Barnes kills Elias, Barnes runs back to the remaining men: 'Elias is dead. Gooks all over the place.' But as they are choppered out, Elias appears running, and shot. He is on his knees, his arms flung out in a simulacrum of the crucified Christ.

As soon as they arrived in the Philippines, the actors were sent on an intensive two-week 'training course'. Living in the jungle, they were prey to forced marches, digging foxholes, even night ambushes complete with special-effects explosions. In typical military manner Stone was trying to break them down, or, as he told *New York* magazine, 'to fuck with their heads so we could get that dog-tired, don't-give-a-damn attitude, the anger, the irritation, the casual way of brutality, the casual approach to death. What I remember most about being there and what a lot of guys remember is just the tiredness.'

Platoon took 54 days to shoot and cost six and a half million dollars: some 15 per cent of the script was dropped in the edit. A deal was struck with the Philippine military to use their military equipment, as had been done for *Apocalypse Now*, filmed in the same country.

Without the comic absurdity of *Salvador*, *Platoon* was a far more sombre film; there was a sense of distance that could be felt from the first measured, observing words of Charlie Sheen's voice-over. The epic story of Vietnam from the American grunt point-of-view was told from this resonating microcosmic perspective. And there was an elegiac, mournful quality to the pacing of the editing and Bob Richardson's lingering camera sweeps: to some extent the film was like a period piece.

Oliver Stone, however, hadn't held back on any of the details of his own experience in Vietnam. For example, the village atrocity scene is a pivotal moment in which Chris Taylor has a moment in which he loses control, and comes very close to wantonly shooting a villager, firing around his feet and making him dance. Then he catches himself, and a change is wrought in his character. Again, Stone based this on fact, on something he had done himself. 'I almost blew the gook away, when I made him dance...I mean, I could have gotten away with it. I could have fuckin' killed him, and nobody would have busted me,' he told *Playboy*.

In the same scene, in the same hut, Bunny, played by Kevin Dillon, doesn't indicate any urgings of an inner voice, or if he does hear it, it is ignored. Caving in a woman's skull with his rifle-butt, he laughs with glee as her brains spill out. 'There were random killings. Nothing ever

On the set of Platoon, shot in the Philippines, Stone felt distant from the making of the film; he had tried for so long to get the autobiographical script made that now it felt like a 'duty'.

preordained, nothing ordered. It would be like we'd go to a village; Bunny, for example – the Kevin Dillon character – he really killed that woman. He battered her. He smashed her head with the stock of a '16, burned her hooch down, but it was in an isolated part of the village. Nobody saw it.' Later in the same scene, Chris stops three other infantry-men from raping a young girl.

At the end of the film, in his final voice-over, Chris Taylor ponders on his Vietnam experience:

> I think now, looking back, we did not fight the enemy, we fought ourselves – and the enemy was in us... The war is over for me now, but it will always be there – the rest of my days. As I am sure Elias will be – fighting with Barnes for possession of my soul... There are times when I have felt like the child born of those two fathers...but be that as it may, those of us who did make it have an obligation to build again, to teach to others what we know, and to try with what's left of our lives to find a goodness and a meaning to this life.

It is as though we are listening to the personal credo of Oliver Stone – which we almost certainly are.

The film's lugubrious atmosphere – enhanced by the way in which scenes slide into each other – makes it feel like an epitaph to the wasted lives and years of the Vietnam war. When it opened on 19 December 1986, initially only in six theatres, to build a word-of-mouth buzz, it showed instantly that it had hit a core nerve of heartland America. At 11.30 in the morning there were lines around the block in New York. In the *New York Times* Vincent Canby described *Platoon* as 'a major piece of work'. It was, he said in high praise, 'possibly the best work of any kind about Vietnam since Michael Herr's book *Dispatches*.' In *New York* magazine David Denby described *Platoon* as 'a great American movie', adding that 'Oliver Stone completes his amazing transformation from bum to hero.' On the West Coast Sheila Benson wrote in the *Los Angeles Times* that 'War movies of the past, even the greatest ones, seem like crane shots by comparison. *Platoon* is at ground zero.' She compared Oliver Stone's direction to being 'like a Goya with a camera'.

By the beginning of February 1987 *Platoon* was the number one box-office hit in the USA. More than that, its autobiographical elements and ring of truth rendered it a phenomenon. The film's success brought up discussion of the Vietnam war that had long lain dormant. *Platoon* took $136 million at the US box office and received eight Acadamy Award nominations and four Oscars, including Best Picture, Best Director, Best Screenplay, and Best Cinematography. This success helped focus atten-tion on Stone's previous film: with co-writer Richard Boyle, Oliver Stone was also nominated for Best Screenplay for *Salvador*, meaning that he was competing against himself; meanwhile, James Woods was nominated as Best Actor for his portrayal of Boyle. *Salvador*, however, won neither of the categories.

> There could be no greater moment in my life [said Stone, describing those Academy Awards on 30 March 1987]. It was like an expurgation. Everything had come round. By being different, by being the underdog, by going to Vietnam, by being ignored, by being shitted on, by having the script rejected so many times...it was all a circle come round and true. The film got made, I directed it at the end of the day. I directed what I wrote. It wins the Academy Award. It becomes a worldwide phenomenon. I'm known everywhere for this movie based on my life. It's one of those miracles of life.
>
> *Platoon* was as good as it gets. Yeah, you can say there's another night where you finally sleep with the woman of your dreams. There's this incredible evening here.... And there's all these fantasies that come true in our lives if you're out there as I am; I'm an adventurer, I put myself on the line; I've had horrible times, but I've also had great times.
>
> But that was, in the movie parlance of the day, as good as it will ever be. And I always remember it fondly. But I'll never chase it. Because it can never be the same again. My life has taken other forms.

Did he feel cynical that he was getting these Academy Awards from people who had previously rejected him? Or did he simply feel justified?

> Of course I did. I didn't realize it was such a political process as I do now. But at that time I felt very justified and validated. And happy. Incredibly happy. It was a fairy-tale come true. I wished that I'd looked better. I wish I'd been a few years younger. I wish I hadn't stressed out so much, because I went through a lot of hell in that period. Making *Platoon* was a very hard movie too physically. I was tired, beat-up. I wish I'd taken better care of myself along the way. Because I neglected a lot of my physical side to work hard. As a writer and as a director, I really neglected a lot of myself.
>
> So at that point in my life I paid a little more attention to myself. Get a manicure, get some decent clothes, start to live a life a bit. Breathe. Have children. Look around you. Buy a house. All those great things that start to happen and you think, 'Isn't this great?'.... until you get in deeper and deeper and realize it's a materialistic hellhole.' [He laughs at length.]

5 Wall Street

In his next film Oliver Stone dealt with the broader implications of that materialistic hellhole.

Wall Street was a brave, unexpected film that again indicated the director was intuitively in touch with the *zeitgeist*. Shot in New York in the spring and summer of 1987, it dealt with the central theme of its era, the extraordinary worship of gross materialism that emanated from dark role models working in the financial powerhouses of the world; a philosophy that in Black October that year was to result in the biggest financial crash since that of 1929. Consciously or unconsciously, Stone drew attention to the thinking that led to the tragedies of El Salvador and Vietnam, as though *Wall Street* was the final film in a trilogy.

No one died in *Wall Street*; there were no machine-guns; and there was more dialogue in the screenplay than in any other previous Oliver Stone film. In fact, *Wall Street* was very different from *Salvador* and *Platoon*, because it wasn't about a black-and-white world but more about the shades of grey, the movements in the shadows. The film even showed that there could be a 'good' capitalist. Speaking to Alexander Cockburn, Stone said that, contrary to the media's impression of him, he was extremely ambivalent: 'In movies and plays, a black-and-white outlook is very dangerous.'

Wall Street was inspired by his broker father, a film-lover with whom he would go to see quality films like *Dr Strangelove*, *Paths of Glory*, and *Seven Days in May*. Almost invariably Lou Stone would comment afterwards, 'We could've done it better, Huckleberry.'

Dad used to love to take in those movies and he loved to talk about what was real [Stone told me]. And he would say, 'There's no good business movies, Oliver.' That's what provoked me. So I wanted to do that, and make one against the grain that would be a good business movie. Isn't that a strange idea? [Laughs.]

Set in 1985, the film was dedicated to Lou Stone. Oliver Stone's father had been a liberal Republican who believed in capitalism with a passion. Ironically, he had owned few possessions: homes, cars were all rented.

'There was an insecurity at the heart of our family existence,' Stone told *Premiere* magazine in December 1987. 'I began to resent money as the criterion by which to judge all things, and there grew to be a raging battle between my father and me about it. I found ways to throw away everything I had, which pissed my father off.'

All the same, Stone admitted,

> my father taught me how to write. He said writing is ass plus seat. Basically, it's very hard work. But nobody deals with screenwriters as if they're serious writers. They're always looked down upon, which is bullshit... I'm always scared of writing. I always fret before I write a screenplay, get very nervous, very insecure. Writing is extremely antisocial. I get into a very depressed mode.

In the film the paternal Hal Holbrook played the part of the voice of an older Wall Street that was specifically that of the director's father.

> *Wall Street* was paying an homage to Dad [Oliver Stone said]. And it was also asking, 'Look, can I do other things beside war and documentary type films? Can I take another style and go back into the old, very limited tradition of the business movie?' Which I was always interested in because my Dad was a businessman, a very astute one.
>
> The Wall Street that my father worked in, the one I grew up around, was wholly different from that of today. There were no computers; they didn't trade in such volume; there were fixed commissions...He'd explain to me what business is. The business of America, Calvin Coolidge said, is business. He made me aware of what serious business is.
>
> My father believed that America's business brought peace to the world and built industry through science and research, and that capital is needed for that. But this idea seems to have been perverted to a large degree. I don't think my father would recognize America today.

The story of *Wall Street* is that of an ambitious young commodities trader, Bud Fox (Charlie Sheen), who is prepared to follow any course to become rich. He has no qualms about insider trading and buys his way into the good books of Gordon Gekko (a masterly performance by Michael Douglas) by slipping him tips. Disguised as a member of a cleaning force, he trawls through office files of companies ripe for corporate raids, passing on the information to Gekko. His downfall occurs when he goes too far: he tips off Gekko that the company for which his father (Martin Sheen) works, Blue Star Airlines, is ripe for a corporate raid. As Elias and Barnes had vied for his soul in *Platoon*, here Charlie Sheen's cinematic and actual father (Martin Sheen) and Gordon Gekko, the investment raider, played out the same opposing roles.

Stone works with Darryl Hannah and Charlie Sheen on Wall Street**, his excoriating critique of Yuppie mores.**

I wasn't trying to rip off *Platoon* with the character of young Sheen. People misunderstood that. That was a kid of that time, sort of a kid of easy morals. Like kids do: they slide, they don't have big morals. He kind of slides easily into it. And at the end he kind of realizes it. And he comes out of it. That's the idea.

In essence *Wall Street* is a *Pilgrim's Progress* story, Stone told *American Film*'s Alexander Cockburn:

of a boy who is seduced, corrupted, by the allure of easy money. And in the third act, he sets out to redeem himself. He goes back to an essential decency that he rediscovers in himself – very much like some of us do in life. Pointing to myself, I can say that I went through a period of heavy drug usage. I came out of it and wrote *Scarface* cold turkey. It was like a farewell to cocaine.

Cockburn countered that you don't see much of people recovering their moral balance on the real Wall Street.

Well, that brings us to the essential point of what movies are and how they function. More and more, I feel that movies are not reality, but an approximation of reality, and, in some cases, a wish fulfilment. It's an eternal human quality: the need to believe in something better. Life doesn't often work out that way, but movies do.

The oleaginous Gordon Gekko is as powerful and idiosyncratic as the Richard Boyle character had been in *Salvador*. With his greased-back hair and tailored suits, this reptilian figure is one of the great cinematic characters of the Eighties. He lives by the code of Sun Tzu's *The Art of War*, the Bible of many Eighties *laissez-faire* capitalists: his language is peppered with militaristic terminology, specifically the need to make 'killings'. His 'greed is good' speech, to the stockholders of Teldar Paper, which he acquired through subterfuge, is one of the great soliloquies in modern cinema. Gekko's world is one of financial machismo. 'Lunch is for wimps,' he announces, addressing all and sundry as 'pal' when he might as well use the word 'victim'.

Stone wrote the script with an old friend, Stanley Weiser, who studied such fascinating stockmarket buccaneers as Sir James Goldsmith, Carl Icahn, and Asher Edelman. Meanwhile, David Brown, a broker who had been convicted of insider trading, served as an adviser on the film.

I'm ambivalent [Stone told Alexander Cockburn in his interview for *American Film*]. Half of me likes what they do because they shake up entrenched management bureaucracies. I'm generally on the side of the noncorporate types. I don't want to make the raider character in the film a big ugly cat. You like what Michael Douglas does – like Sergeant Barnes in *Platoon*.

Gekko was based on a friend Stone had had in New York in 1981. The same age as Oliver Stone at the time, the man was a multimillionaire from commodities transactions. On the phone 16 to 18 hours a day, he had had a spectacular beach house in Bridgehampton, and, as if that was not enough, an even larger house a few miles down the road. 'It was very Gatsbyesque. I have a line in *Wall Street*: "Money never sleeps."'

The man's lifestyle, Stone said, was 'Scarface north'.

This guy was the New York version of what was going down in Miami, where people were hyperconsuming. Wall Street is the equivalent of the cocaine trade in some ways... My friend got more and more money until inevitably he reached a point when it just blew up in his face. He started to make mistakes, and one of his mistakes cost him everything. He was forced to reassess everything in life.

The budget for *Wall Street* was over $15 million, beyond the financial scope of Hemdale. With Ed Pressman on board as producer, 20th Century Fox went for Oliver Stone's idea. For the studio it was a medium-budget movie.

In pre-production the director worked out of an office on the 20th Century Fox lot. He was now into art, collecting pieces by Julian Schnabel and Andy Warhol.

As usual Oliver Stone had done his research, and went about getting his actors into character with his by now habitual assiduity. Although *The Wall Street Journal* turned him down when he asked to shoot in their offices, Charlie Sheen and Michael Douglas spent time inside Salomon Brothers, the prestigious brokers, thanks to Ken Lipper, the firm's managing director, a former deputy mayor of New York, who had been taken on as a consultant. Most importantly, Lipper persuaded the New York Stock Exchange to let Stone film there, to the irritation of many older traders, interrupted in their course of money-making.

There is a devilish side to Charlie that didn't come out in Platoon [Stone said of Charlie Sheen to Premiere magazine], where he was more of an idealized figure. I think he's been in trouble, and that shows in his personality, a strong streak of rebelliousness combined with an inner grace passed on from his father, Martin Sheen, who plays his father in the film.

Oliver Stone wasn't the only person involved with the film who was responding to a paternal influence: this was the first time that Michael Douglas had played the bad guy. 'He told me at one point that his Dad had implied that he was finally about to become a real actor, that he had always played wimps, and that this was a role where he could play more towards his father, who could do a heel as well as a hero. Michael loved that idea.'

Stone was surprised by the nervousness exhibited by Douglas in the first days of shooting. On day one Stone gave him three pages of monologue to perform, and Douglas had a hard time with such a start. But 'by the time we got to the scenes in his office, he was on top of his game.'

Daryl Hannah, however, was much criticized. Stone saw that she was having difficulty with her part as Charlie Sheen's love interest – she is also the mistress of the Michael Douglas character – and felt that at times she wanted to quit.

> I think I made her cry a few times, but I wasn't really pleased with her wanness and passiveness, which were difficult to get through.
>
> Now I would improve certain things in the script [Stone told me]. But we rushed it a bit, because we wanted to take advantage of that timing. I would have done it a little differently. I still have a problem with the script on my Daryl Hannah character. There was a better way to do it. I see it now.

A large number of moving camera shots from Bob Richardson (whom Alex Cox had tried to steal away for *Walker*, his Nicaragua story) were used in *Wall Street* 'because we are making a movie about sharks, about feeding frenzies, so we wanted the camera to become a predator. There is no let-up until you get to the fixed world of Charlie's father, where the stationary camera gives you a sense of immutable values.' When the camera was on Charlie Sheen, it was energetic, nervy, almost as though he was on coke.

Wall Street was a 53-day shoot. Stone came in seven days ahead of schedule and $2 million under budget, partially because he was racing to finish shooting before an expected strike call by the Directors Guild. 'We never wasted an hour. If it rained we made it a rain scene: Charlie goes to the beach in the rain.'

Oliver Stone had already predicted the critical response to his latest film. 'I would rather turn out something fast, get it over with, give the gold crown to somebody else so I can get on with doing things that I really care about, which are ideas. I'm ready to take a fall.' But had Oliver Stone really understood the rules of the game? Not quite, it seemed.

> That was the most well-placed film. Although it was a complicated movie, it was not a simplistic movie. It had a lot of jargon in it. Like *Platoon* had a lot of jargon. It was detailed. Unfortunately, the reviewers were looking to destroy the picture. I remember the headline in the *LA Times* at the time: 'Wall Street Lays An Egg.' The headline was far worse than the review, but obviously they were looking to

get the Golden Boy from the year before. I was an outsider to this game. In some ways, I still think I don't know how to play it that well. But I didn't realize the degree of spite and jealousy. That it's a game unto itself.

With the critics, Oliver Stone's two-picture honeymoon was over. The review in the *Los Angeles Times* set the tone. The emotional dynamics and slow burn of the film were largely overlooked. Previously loyal Stone supporters like Vincent Canby considered that 'the movie crashes in a heap of platitudes that remind us that honesty is after all the best policy... Even at its best, *Wall Street* is an uneven struggle. At its worst, it's a muddle.'

The *LA Weekly*'s John Powers, who had applauded *Salvador*, turned the virtues he had previously spotted in Stone's work into vices:

Stone's a pulp film-maker whose coarsest excesses are probably inseparable from his most flamboyant virtues. *Wall Street* has the jacked-up quality you find in Sam Fuller or Jim Thompson: the swatches of undergraduate dialogue ('Who am I?' Bud wonders aloud), the speed-freak camera style (Stone even uses whiplash pans for a conversation in an elevator), the stupefying incomprehension of women (Stone's usual assortment of tramps and bimbos)...

Like Lou Stone, *Wall Street* was really of another age: a moral movie of the sort once delivered by Frank Capra, with an acute, pointed use of histrionics that might have been scripted by Theodore Dreiser. In *New York* magazine David Denby understood:

A sensationally entertaining melodrama about greed and corruption in New York...*Wall Street*, a gleeful send-up of the culture of money, rarely averts its rapt attention from the gross yet also mystical and delicate issue of dollar value – not just of stocks but of paintings, decor, and even personal relationships.

Oliver Stone, however, had the last laugh. *Wall Street* took in over $100 million worldwide, and in the 1987 Academy Awards Michael Douglas won the Oscar for Best Actor.

You read about these kids who are making a million bucks, two million bucks a year – it demoralizes the person making $40,000 a year [said Stone]. All of a sudden everybody needs a Porsche or a VCR or a fishing boat. And that is what fuels America, more and more greed. We deal with these issues by staying inside a very small story, one fish in one Wall Street aquarium and what happens to that fish.

On 17 September 1987, Oliver Stone had been presented with the Torch of Liberty Award from the American Civil Liberties Union Foundation.

His speech of acceptance contained much of his philosophy of life.

> The forces of war, ignorance, poverty, disease, of Moral Majorityism, fundamentalist religion, of repressive political ideologies – all these are converging to diminish and repress man in the *1984* Orwellian sense of making it more and more difficult for individuals to speak out, to say what they think, what's right and what's wrong.
>
> Our own country has become a military-industrial monolith dedicated to the Cold War, in many ways as rigid and as corrupt at the top as our rivals the Soviets. We have become the enemy – with a security state now second to none. Today we have come to live in total hatred, fear, and the desire to destroy. Bravo. Fear and conformity have triumphed.
>
> Where does a man or woman turn? How do we fight this? What do we do? How can we possibly win against the overwhelming force of this government of the future, this Darth Vadian Empire?
>
> I don't know. I am lost...but somewhere on the back burner of a bewildered mind, I feel I gotta go back to those movies I believed in...where my hero is facing certain extinction surrounded on all sides by enemy swordsmen, but, by some shining light of inner force and greater love, turns the table of fate and triumphs over all odds.

6 Talk Radio

Oliver Stone had been working on the idea of a film called *Contra*: Stone liked the way the word symbolized 'against'. In order to drive home his point, he decided to try to approach it from the point of view of a pair of CIA operatives; Paul Newman was interested in playing the older of the two. 'It's not just about Contras. It's about America being against everything that's progressive.'

Somehow, however, circumstances would not conjoin to let the movie progress. Oliver Stone was obliged to look elsewhere.

On 18 June 1984 a group of right-wing fanatics, incensed by his sneering provocations, had shot dead Alan Berg, a Denver talk-show host as he left his radio studio building. Eric Bogosian, an intense actor and writer, had written a successful New York stage play about a similar killing, in which he starred at Joseph Papp's Public Theatre in 1987. 'I was already working on the play and, through some strange coincidence, the fictional character I was making up was very much like the real-life Alan Berg,' Bogosian told me.

'Shock-jocks' Howard Stern and Morton Downey Jr. were also used as source material for Barry Champlain, the fictional talk-show host created by Bogosian who, in the specialized manner of the genre, would endlessly abuse and harangue his listeners.

This 'shock' radio style had become a national phenomenon in the United States during the Eighties. Wilfully, almost neurotically populist, the hosts histrionically offered themselves as the personification of the Common Man: they said what was on their mind, they proudly proclaimed, which meant they had a right to be as insensitive, belligerent, and offensive as humanly possible about religion, sex, politics, racial matters, or any other potentially touchy areas. In an increasingly PC age, they were The Anti-PC.

By turns cajoling, dismissive, or bonding with the callers to their programmes, they set themselves up as lone voices of sanity, a throwback to tub-thumping newspaper columnists in an increasingly non-literate age.

Ed Pressman had bought the option to Bogosian's play; a prime reason for buying it was his insistence that Bogosian should play the role of Barry Champlain. Oliver Stone met Eric Bogosian at a Los Angeles screening of *Wall Street* in the late summer of 1987 and got on with him immediately; Pressman asked him to come on board the production of *Talk Radio* as co-producer. Stone now believes, however, that Pressman hoped that by getting him involved in the project he would eventually want to direct it. Pressman had bought the rights to *Talked to Death*, a book written by Stephen Singular about the events leading to Berg's killing. Incorporating this material into the original 90-minute stage play, Bogosian worked on a film script based around his original text.

> When it came to make the film [said Bogosian], we used a lot of biographical information from Berg – some of Berg's story – to add more drama to the story that I had already created for the stage. I think that the drama is the same story, essentially. The show is going national. It gets very out-of-hand on this one particular night, and things get out of control for Barry. It's the same story, but we added some things.

After delivering a first draft in October 1987, Bogosian, at Stone's urging, substantially rewrote the screenplay whilst on a Christmas vacation in Australia. 'When Oliver and I didn't agree, sometimes we'd trade off. If sometimes I'd say, "I just can't say this line," he'd say, "Well, I just can't have you say that line." So I'd say, "Alright, I'll say your line, if you accept my line," and this would be the way we'd get things settled.'

By the time Eric Bogosian had returned to the United States at the end of January, Oliver Stone was on board as director. The budget was $4 million and a 25-day shoot was scheduled.

For the sake of dramatic possibilities it was decreed that – unlike real radio hosts – Bogosian would wear a radio headset to allow him to wander around the studio, reducing the number of static scenes. Art director Bruno Rubeo turned a Dallas warehouse into a fully equipped radio station: Texas permits non-union film crews and would also be used for the making of *Born on the Fourth of July* and *JFK*. Indeed, Eric Bogosian claimed that it was the build-up to Oliver Stone's second Vietnam film that lay behind the making of *Talk Radio* in the first place. 'What he wanted to do was basically pop off a movie while he was prepping *Born on the Fourth of July*. It was unbelievable.'

But weren't there other motives as well as artistic ones? In fact, *Talk Radio* was extremely lucrative for Oliver Stone. When Garth Drabinski, the Canadian owner of Cineplex Odeon, came looking to buy the rights to a Stone film, the director sold him them for $10 million. After $4 million had been spent on making the film, Stone and Ed Pressman split the remaining $6 million between them. 'That was the biggest deal I ever made,' said Stone.

Talk Radio is set in the penthouse studio of KGAB, a fictional Dallas radio station. Chuck Deitz, a representative of Metrowave, a radio broadcast corporation, visits the station to discuss the possibility of the imminent national syndication of Barry Champlain's *Night Talk* show: 'You're listening to the best talk in Texas – Barry Champlain on KTAB! The lines are open!'

The deal is dependent, however, on Champlain's willingness to dilute his more extreme opinions. On the air that night Champlain plays his part to the max: 'This country is in deep trouble, people, this country is rotten to the core... Tell me what to do about the mess this country's in!'

This is the first that Champlain has heard of the possibility of his show going nationwide ('So it's a hot show. Stu, find me a catheter, will ya?'). He announces this to his listeners: 'They asked me if I wanted to soften my touch, go easier. I told them to take it or leave it. Monday, we begin national broadcasting. You better have something to say – I know I do.'

> When this man finds out that he has a potential audience of hundreds of thousands of people, maybe even larger, if he goes national [said Bogosian], his fear is changed into excitement at the possibility of connecting with all these people. I think every performer tries to connect with an audience in a way that they can't connect with people on a day-to-day basis.

As his evening show progresses, Champlain debates the matter with the station manager (Alec Baldwin). He also phones and invites his ex-wife Ellen (Ellen Greene) to come to Dallas the next weekend after telling her the news. His girlfriend, Laura (Leslie Hope), who works at the station, is unaware of this. A racist claims to have mailed him a bomb ('Chet, so nice to hear from you again! Shouldn't you be out burning crosses or molesting children or something?'): when the package is opened it contains a dead rat.

When Ellen arrives for the weekend, Laura, who is at Champlain's apartment when she calls from the airport, is distressed by her visit. Ellen tells Champlain he has to begin to love himself and to have a relationship with someone with a soul. A flashback shows his past as a salesman in a menswear store, where an older man notices him and has him on his radio show as a guest. We see Ellen faking calls to her husband's first shows to boost his popularity.

Back in Dallas at a basketball game Barry Champlain is booed by the audience.

At the beginning of the next week, supposedly the first day of his show going nationwide, the Chicago syndication network announces that it has temporarily postponed this until they are certain Champlain has renounced his more extreme audience abuse.

In his show that night Champlain is more outrageous than ever. When a cab-driver caller says that the shock jock needs to be hit, Champlain responds by saying 'the way you hit your little girls?': he tells the cabbie that his wife's a hooker, his brother a pimp. A rapist says he's about to strike again – Champlain tries to get the call traced but fails.

He agrees to the call from Kent, a druggy teenager, to come on the show live. Kent arrives at the studio and talks in white rocker babble, laughing, agreeing, when Champlain tells him he is an idiot.

Ellen calls again, pretending to be just another phone-in addict. Speaking in code, she lets her ex-husband know she still loves him and wants him back. Barry Champlain tells her to go buy a heavy-duty vibrator. 'You blew it. Your ex doesn't want you.'

Closing his show with an extraordinary soliloquy, Champlain tells his audience of his own hypocrisy. 'I denounce the system and I embrace it. I want money and power and prestige. I want ratings and success and I don't give a damn about you or the world.'

Such forthrightness impresses Metrowave's Chuck Deitz. As Champlain leaves the studio he announces he's ready to go nationwide.

Heading for his car, Barry Champlain is approached by an overweight, middle-aged man who asks for his autograph. Then he shoots him several times.

This extensively verbal film was entirely different from Oliver Stone's three previous movies, each of which were in their own way very separate from each other. However, *Salvador*, *Platoon*, and *Wall Street* had been played out on large panoramas, whose locations were part of a larger visual choreography. By contrast, *Talk Radio* was almost a chamber piece, an art house film, in which the voices of the various callers to Barry Champlain provided the majority of the other characters. Bob Richardson's use of dark lighting gave the film a look that was intensely *noir*. And the film spoke with a directness of attack that hung on Bogosian's riveting performance and script.

> I had to work with only six actors in a very confined space [said Stone]. How do we make that space work for us? How do we make dialogue work? All those questions were in the forefront. And I think I'm very happy with the film. I succeeded in what I did. I learned a lot from it. It was for me, I suppose, the equivalent of working on a stage play.

Oliver Stone, pausing for thought during the making of Talk Radio.

How exactly does Oliver Stone work with actors? How hands-on is he?

> I think with actors you try to... A director has to be humble. I think that he has to listen to them, he has to feel where they're leading to, to try and help them in some way, but not by dictating, but by listening and guiding, and making suggestions, but by doing it in a way that the actor feels that it's his.
>
> I think that directing actors is a very humbling experience. People have this image of directors as martinets with a whip – it doesn't work that way at all. It's more the reverse, that you have to listen to everybody's gripes and everybody's fears. I mean, it's pretty exhausting, but through the medium, through the director, I think something happens, something grows, like in a petrie dish.

(Lest there be any niggling suspicion of false modesty in Stone's reply, it is worth hearing the witness voice of James Woods writing on this matter: 'He achieves his desired end as a film-maker by being provocative and yet at the same time subverting his own ego in the process. For Oliver Stone nothing matters but the film and the result that even he may not consciously know he is seeking. Some deep intuition drives him, a majestic demon muse to whom he is but a humble servant.')

A clear sideways step to give Oliver Stone breathing-space, *Talk Radio* remains a fascinating curio. Yet another look at the underbelly of the United States, it deals with some of the same subject-matter that would later be considered to more chilling effect in *Natural Born Killers*: there is a clear link between the audience manipulations of Barry Champlain and those of Wayne Gale in the later film: for both those characters there are questions of male identity and professional probity. Champlain is the archetype of the narcissistic media star, communicating with others because he is unable to communicate with himself, about whom he knows little. *Talk Radio* is a burst of energy, symbolized by its short shoot, that still stands on its own.

Critical response, however, was decidedly mixed. David Denby saw it as 'one of the most complete expressions of paranoia ever put on film.... Bogosian and Stone are a dreadnought combination: they produce enough anxiety to throw a ten-ton tank into depression. And *Talk Radio*, though exciting, isn't really exhilarating. It's too overwrought to give much pleasure.'

However, the *New York Times*'s Vincent Canby didn't go along with it, comparing it unfavourably to the stage play. 'Mr Bogosian repeats his stage performance as Barry with a lot of furious energy but no real pay-off. He keeps being interrupted by the dopey demands of the dreadful screenplay...a nearly perfect example of how not to make a movie from a play.' And in *Time* magazine Richard Corliss complained, 'This is bag lady cinema.'

'*Talk Radio* had very mixed reviews,' said Oliver Stone, 'some very ugly reviews in major publications that hurt, but one hopes that the film will last.'

In many quarters the worth and weight of the film were recognized. At the 1989 Berlin Film Festival, for example, Eric Bogosian won the Silver Bear for Outstanding Single Achievement. 'One year ago, around this time,' he said in his acceptance speech, 'I went to Oliver Stone's house to discuss the script and casting. He took me back to his study – he had two Oscars and a Golden Bear sitting there. I picked up the Golden Bear, and I had no idea that one year later I would be holding a bear in my hands. Thank you.'

Talk Radio is the darkest film I've made [Oliver Stone later told *Time* magazine], but I don't personally feel that way about America. I have a lot more hope for America. I see it as a totally homogenous land, and I love its vastness and its freedom... If anything, in my work I've tried to veer away from the elites that I think have corrupted and made cynical the American Dream. I hark back to an immigrant belief in the goodness of this country. I find it coming still from Asia, Mexico, Latin America, Europe. I think movies in a sense thrive on that democracy.

7 Born on the Fourth of July

In 1987 Paula Wagner, Oliver Stone's agent, mentioned to him that she thought he might revive the *Born on the Fourth of July* project. This time, of course, he would be the director. It was to be a reversal of fortune at a level that was almost metaphysical: so bitter had been the recriminations between Stone and Kovic over the previous failure to make the film that at one point Kovic had punched the screenwriter, in a parking lot in Los Angeles.

> I had made *Platoon* as a universal movie in many ways [he told me]. But because I came from a more privileged social class, my return home was not the same as the usual veteran who'd been through combat. I was working on an idea about my homecoming and I'd written the script: twice, in fact – it was called *Second Life*. But I never was satisfied with it. And I thought compared to Ron's story...Ron told a much larger story about the extreme of the returning veteran story. And perhaps that was the right way to do it, to do the extreme.

Wagner, moreover, was also the agent for the new heartthrob star Tom Cruise, and she suggested him for the part of Kovic. Glancing at his career up until then, he seemed an unlikely candidate for a part that required such intensity and variety of emotion. Although he had had a relatively distinguished role opposite Paul Newman in *The Colour of Money*, his career seemed more represented by his lead part in the gung-ho *Top Gun* (the antithesis of the spirit of *Born on the Fourth of July*) or the deeply crass *Cocktail*. He was about to embark, however, on a role that would stretch him far more – playing the straight man to Dustin Hoffman's idiot savant in *Rain Man*.

Unsurprisingly, Kovic was initially unconvinced by the idea of Cruise playing him. Yet when he met him he experienced an empathy he had never felt with Al Pacino; their birthdays were only a day apart, for example: Ron Kovic really was born on 4 July, whilst Tom Cruise was born on 3 July.

Similarly, Stone had also considered Charlie Sheen yet again for the part, as well as Sean Penn and Nicolas Cage; but he soon came down on the side of Cruise.

> There was a similarity between him and Kovic [he said], wanting to be the best, being competitive, being the winner – number one. Very much the same mentality. And I thought that would be usable. The question in my mind as a director was simply how I would cross him over once he had become a paraplegic...the new territory for Tom. But that's where we explored his vulnerabilities. Certainly he was exposed to wheelchairs and Kovic a lot. And we really tried to put a darker stain on his jock image.

The scope of the film made it Oliver Stone's largest picture yet. It covered plenty of territory, emotionally, thematically, geographically: Kovic's childhood in and traumatized return to Massapequa, Long Island; war sequences in Vietnam; binges in Mexico; rejection and redemption at the 1972 Republican and the 1976 Democratic conventions.

And although the budget that Universal had given him was close to that of *Wall Street* – $14 million – it had to stretch a long way: the cast had 160 speaking roles and 1,200 extras. There was a sense in Hollywood, moreover, that Stone seemed to be re-treading former ground with another Vietnam film. Steeling himself against such a mood, the director soldiered on, mustering an impressive cast that included some actors from *Platoon*, notably Willem Dafoe and Tom Berenger in cameo parts. Harking back to his days working on *Year of the Dragon*, Stone chose two of that film's players, Raymond J. Barry and Caroline Kava, to take the roles of Kovic's parents.

The story of *Born on the Fourth of July* – Ron Kovic's story – is that of an Everyman who becomes an archetype. The film begins in the naïve Cold War, post-World War II days of the 1950s with a group of boys playing with toy guns in a John Wayne world: simple but telling brushstrokes. The patriotism of the Fourth of July parade in 1957 in Massapequa, Long Island, is shown up for its dangerous blindness by the appearance of veterans in wheelchairs. Ten years later Ron Kovic joins the marines. 'Communism's got to be stopped', his mother says endorsing his decision. 'It's God's will you go.'

After his platoon has mistakenly shot up a village of Vietnamese women and children, Kovic shoots at a blurred figure: it is another American soldier, who drops, mortally wounded. When he tries to tell an officer what he's done, the response is to the point: 'I don't want anyone coming to me with this shit. Carry on.'

In another firefight Ron Kovic is shot in the chest and is given the last rites.

Oliver Stone with Ron Kovic, the paraplegic author of Born on the Fourth of July.

Back in the USA, Kovic is 'treated' at the rat-infested Bronx Veterans Hospital. In some of the most harrowing scenes in modern cinema, he learns that he will never walk again, never have children. He discovers that the black orderlies consider Vietnam to be a white man's war that doesn't concern them; and that the government seems to almost feel the same: the pump on Kovic's leg dressing stops working because of a lack of funds.

Ron, however, remains a patriot. Even back at his parents' home in Massapequa, he quarrels with his brother. 'You want to burn the flag? Love it or leave it.'

Soon, however, he cracks up and rolls home in his wheelchair drunk. In a heartbreaking fight with his mother, she shows the thinking that brainwashed him into coming home from Vietnam with a destroyed body. 'We got a drunk for a son,' she complains, telling him he needs help.

'*You* need help, with your God and your bullshit dreams about me. Fuck you!... There's no God, no country: just me in this wheelchair and this dead penis.'

'Don't say penis in this house,' is her reply.

As though he is a manifestation of their unrealized guilt, Ron Kovic has become an embarrassment to all who once knew him in repressed, uptight Massapequa – and, by extension, the United States. In Ron Kovic the illusions that inform that society, on which it in fact depends, have been stripped away, revealing its grim core.

Travelling down to Mexico, Ron discovers a colony of disabled vets. These men are his soul-mates; they understand what happened. 'Fuck the States!' proclaims Charlie (Willem Dafoe). By a roadside in the desert, Ron and Charlie argue insanely and fight, their barely repressed anger exploding from them.

After this catharsis, Ron Kovic travels up to Georgia and confesses to the parents of the boy he killed.

By the time of the 1972 Republican Convention in Miami, Ron Kovic is radicalized. With other vets he protests outside the convention hall, being thrown from his wheelchair by security guards for his efforts.

By the 1976 Democratic Convention, however, matters have turned around. Ron Kovic is a guest speaker. His mother's voice momentarily interrupts: 'I had a dream that you were speaking to a large group of people, and that you were saying great things.'

Oliver Stone began shooting *Born on the Fourth of July* in October 1988. Although the budget was not high, enormous achievements had been made with it.

Bruno Rubeo was my art director at the time. He always did a great job with what we had. We always did great naturalistic stuff using little money. We built Long

Island in Texas – it looks great: Massapequa with no money – a great job. In the Philippines he built a Mexican village. We were always masters at that, at camouflaging what you've got.

It was a 65-day shoot, and Ron Kovic was on the set almost every day, becoming extremely distressed on occasions, notably during the fight between himself and his mother.

Born on the Fourth of July is a modern epic to me [said Stone]. About a mass of people with ugly furniture. Not about castles and kings. But Mr and Mrs America at home. Mom and the wheelchair. When I went to Massapequa everything was small. It struck me that Ronnie was living in a baby room. So I built the house a little bit bigger on a sound stage. But we built it narrower. And I used a lo-mo steadicam, which had very rarely been done that extensively. We were whipping down these halls...but it's a small house. So by putting the wheelchair wide in this small house we got a sense of largeness there. And the framing is all done very claustrophically.

The Vietnam stuff was wholly different stylistically from the *Platoon* stuff – as was *Heaven and Earth* later. The hospital work stays in my mind as some of the best work we ever did. Very tough.

Editing was not easy. For both expedience and a varied energy, Oliver Stone employs several editors and lets them work on each other's scenes. But the shooting-up of the Vietnamese village, for example, simply wouldn't come together until Stone opted to try a cinéma-vérité style. And there was even a re-shoot of the final scene at the Democratic Convention. When first shot, it had included all of Kovic's speech. Now it ended as he approached the microphone.

When finally completed and released in December 1989, the emotional impact of *Born on the Fourth of July* was extraordinary. Audiences who surrendered to the film would be reduced to tears at several points.

The writing and direction are such that the mindset at various levels – blue collar working-class innocence, militaristic cynicism, governmental arrogance – that created the Vietnam war is pinpointed so acutely that it produces disgust and rage within the spectator. This emotional impact of the subject-matter affected the director as much as it did the audiences.

I think *Born* is one of the most emotional films I've ever done. I think that the entire structure of the film was dictated by emotions. The editing of the film, the way it was cut, felt... As I remember there were seven or eight valleys and peaks: a lot of emotional work to do. Often people would say afterwards they were

Oliver Stone with Tom Cruise, who gave an extraordinary performance as Ron Kovic in Born on the Fourth of July.

exhausted emotionally. You had to watch that. You learn when to let it go and when not to. When to restrain it.

Much of the film's emotional effect results from a performance by Tom Cruise that is one of the great pieces of acting of recent years.

Tom is a worker [Stone said to me]. Once he accepted the role, he did it with his usual intensity. It was a tough role for him, I think: he'd never done anything like that before. Neither perhaps had I. I'd had the advantage of having seen Pacino do it in rehearsal ten years before. And I'd been around Ron. So I helped him through it. But we were into virgin territory.

Tom wills things to be. I think you'll look back on this film years from now and see him in his youth. That's his youth: it's pretty stark, strong images. Hairstyles, make-up. I think it holds up. I think...it's extraordinary. His work was special. Had he ever done that? No. And I pushed Tom, and I'm sure there were times when he felt he'd snap. Towards the end he was pretty tired. It's a tough role. There was a lot of intensity and I was pushing him. But we were always friendly. But the hospital was the hardest section, the Veterans Hospital in the Bronx.

With a running time of over two hours 20 minutes, this almost epic film was Oliver Stone's longest work to date. 'It was my first long-form. It was much longer originally. I really struggled to cut it down. We had a long ending scene in the Democratic Convention, which was replaced with a short scene. The opening of the film, the boyhood, was much longer. It ended up being a montage.'

As with *Platoon*, Oliver Stone had gone into the shooting of *Born on the Fourth of July* with 'a sense of duty: I think I did it with a sense of obligation'. By the time that editing was completed, however, he experienced another emotion altogether.

I was very proud. I knew this movie was right, because it hit the gut. I had confidence in the movie that it was some of the best work I'd ever done. I felt it was the best overall film. I felt it was better than *Platoon*. Loved showing it because it really moved people. You couldn't help but be affected by the picture if you were in that room, in the screening. It was a very powerful film.

As a kind of counterpoint to its raw power, *Born on the Fourth of July* had its fair share of detractors. Pauline Kael, it seemed, lived in an intellectual version of the enclosed, miserly spirited and naïve Massapequa, unable to go that extra mile – or even to wake up and see clearly. 'It's inconceivable,' she wrote sophisticatedly in the *New Yorker*, 'that Ron Kovic was as innocent as the movie and the 1976 autobiography on which it is based make him out to be. Was this kid kept in a bubble? At some level, everyone knows about the ugliness of war.'

Such elitist, frankly hopeless thinking, of course, was a further explanation of why the war had been allowed to happen. But others understood the picture. Richard Corliss in *Time*, for example: 'The movie's uniqueness is in its tone. Stone plays director as if he were at a cathedral organ with all stops out. Each scene, whether it means to elegize or horrify, is unrelented, unmodulated, rabid with its own righteousness. And yet frequently the crazy machine works because of its voluptuous imagery.'

In *New York*, David Denby wrote that the film was 'relentless but often powerful...a heartbreaking piece of work...Stone and Kovic have consciously created an anti-myth.' And in the *New York Times* Vincent Canby was even more fulsome in his praise: '...a bitter seething postscript to his Oscar-winning *Platoon*. It is a film of enormous visceral power, with, in the central role, a performance by Tom Cruise that defines everything that is best about the movie. He is both particular and emblematic. He is innocent and clean-cut at the start; at the end, angry and exhausted...'

But how did the social historians see it? The usual shit: Stone was criticized on points of detail. As a kind of conceptual conceit he had used the real Abbie Hoffman for a brief cameo, showing him at an anti-war demonstration at Syracuse University; Hoffman, it was rabidly pointed out, had never visited Syracuse – which was hardly the point.

More crucially, the director was attacked for having manufactured the scene in which Ron Kovic visits the family of the Marine he believed he had shot dead. In reality, this had never happened.

There was a huge controversy over that at that time [Stone told me]. I was attacked for – of course! – toying with the truth. Certain people said that his Marine record showed he didn't shoot his own man. But of course the Marine records didn't show that: that was an issue in the film. Ron Kovic to this day is sure that he killed his own man. He's sure of it. The chapter in the book is very clear. He did not go to Georgia, so they really jumped on me for that.

My point was that in a sense it was an exegesis anyway: in writing about it, in confessing it, he was making it public, and admitting guilt and going and asking for confession. So I took that liberty of having him visit the family.

Instead of having the hero at the end of the film sit down and write a book, which is another way I could have done it, I did it the other way. Ron Kovic specifically starts off in the private arena. When he fights with Dafoe in Mexico he realizes he's in hell and he has to change. And he travels to the confession in Georgia. And once he's made that confession it allows him to enter the public arena, which is the finale of the film. He attacks Nixon in Florida and then ends up at the Democratic Convention. In other words, he passes from the private to the public arena – that was the concept of his growth. He became part of history.

In the arena of real life, however, Kovic tried to springboard off the film, perhaps to enlarge his place in history. On the strength of the further publicity it had brought him, he made a pretence of standing for Congress in southern California's Orange County against the right-wing Robert Dornan.

The moment Dornan got threatened by Kovic he started to attack him [remembered Stone]. And the moment he realized attacking a guy in a wheelchair wasn't so bright, then of course he attacked the movie and me. During the whole Academy season. So there was a backlash against Kovic as being seen as an opportunist by people in the industry: all of a sudden he was running for office.

Ron hated Dornan and his politics and had always considered running. But he shouldn't have made that move at that point. He should have waited. And he made the move and he didn't make it. He didn't even announce: he pretended to announce. He got hit both ways. He should have been much lower key politically. I think Ron hurt himself and hurt the building. A tough time, that was a rough one. It was my first real understanding of the politics of film perception: that perception is only in the eye of politics.

After producing five very different films in as many years, films that had altered American cinema for ever, Oliver Stone's honeymoon with the media was over. With *Born on the Fourth of July* he had stumbled into political minefields where the wrath of right-wing pundits was being exploded wherever he trod. All his risk-taking films had been made from the heart, without thought for how the pendulum might swing against him. Now it was beginning to.

Critically, also, he was starting to run into trouble. Oliver Stone's art had always sprung from his instinct; should he have been surprised that for those ruled by their intellects his films were considered an easy target? That he was considered to be emotionally bullying his audience, making downmarket populist fare in which sensationalism was all?

Obviously, I'm aware of that criticism [he told *Rolling Stone*]. Possibly, I go sometimes for the lowest common denominator, in terms of getting the message across, in terms of getting what I want to say across. I think sometimes it's better to be wrong on the side of clarification rather than of obscurity. That's the thing my father used to always beat on me for. Because with all my earlier writing, he'd say, 'That's too obscure.' And all my English teachers would drive me nuts: 'This is too obscure. What do you mean?' Something you've broken your heart writing, that's so clear to you, and nobody understands. And I wrote a lot of obscure stuff. The novel was mostly obscure, it was symbolist poetry, it was Rimbaud-like. I just want to be clear. Maybe part of going the other way is trying to fight all of those earlier tendencies, where I felt like I was totally irrelevant to the human race and that I was totally obscure, and confused.

All the same, the Directors Guild of America named Oliver Stone Best Director of 1989 for *Born on the Fourth of July*; the film was nominated for eight Academy Awards and won two: David Brenner and Joe Hutshing were awarded the Oscar for Best Editing, and Oliver Stone won in the Best Director category, thus making him the only working director to win this Oscar twice; and the film took in over $70 million at the US box office.

8 The Doors

The themes and imagery of *Break*, the first screenplay Oliver Stone had written, were inspired by the music of the Doors. In 1971 Stone had tried to get the script to Jim Morrison, the group's singer, in Paris – but at the time he heard no more of this. Later he was to learn that the screenplay was among the effects found in Morrison's apartment after the singer, songwriter, and poet died in his bath from a heroin overdose. What had Morrison thought of it? Stone wonders to this day.

Oliver Stone felt he had a soul connection with Jim Morrison, that the Doors' frontman was 'like an older brother'. There were parallels in their lives: upper middle-class backgrounds, film school, drug use, a fondness for Paris. The singer with the Doors 'was a shaman. He was a god for me, a Dionysian figure, a poet, a philosopher,' Oliver Stone told the *New York Times*.

Stone shipped out to Vietnam at about the same time as Morrison, the son of a career military officer, was dropping out of UCLA film school. The future film director had first heard the music of the Doors when he was serving in the First Cavalry Division. At the time he was stoned on marijuana. 'The lyrics were very clear. The music was driving and erotic and sinuous – almost Brechtian – and carnivalesque at times, the organ fighting with the guitar. Their first two albums knocked my socks off – that's what the war sounded like to me.' Stone considered songs like 'The End' and 'When The Music's Over' to be epic stories, Homeric ballads.

One of Stone's personal doctrines was based on William Blake's insistence that 'the road of excess leads to the palace of wisdom', a mode of thinking which would appear to have accorded very much with that of Morrison.

Jim had a great line: 'I wasn't mad, I was only interested in freedom.' ...I think he tested every limit that he could find – childhood, parents, the law, women, chemicals, alcohol. Success became a limit, and boredom.

When he was sober or was on other drugs, he would be one of the gentlest souls [said Stone to *Rolling Stone*]. ...he'd go from being the most sensitive, loving, caring person, who talked to everybody – he was very democratic in his approach to life, which I love – and then when he performed, he would go into a shamanistic, devil thing, and then when he was drinking, he would be a monster at times. I also heard that when he was drunk, sometimes he would behave very sweetly. So everybody attests to Jim's kindness. He gave away everything, you know. There was a Jesus quality about his life. He gave of himself: his body, his life, his possessions. Nothing was his. He was a sharing person. It's the Irish dichotomy, I suppose.

The Doors were the definitive Los Angeles group of the second half of the Sixties. Although they only recorded for four years, their tight Gothic sound, married to the supreme confidence and beauty of Morrison's poetic lyrics, along with his suitably enigmatic death in a Paris bathtub in 1971, have made the Doors one of the most legendary of all rock acts.

In 1980 Jerry Hopkins, in collaboration with former Doors' publicist Danny Sugerman, had published *No One Here Gets Out Alive*, a warts-and-all biography of the group. The remaining members of the Doors – keyboard player Ray Manzarek, guitarist Robby Krieger, drummer John Densmore – sold the film rights to their music for $750,000. And in 1988 the Morrison estate offered Carolco all rights to the story. Oliver Stone had a contract with Carolco, and agreed to make the film if he could write the screenplay. This was his first new script since *Wall Street* – and he did it in conjunction with J. Randal Johnson. After some difficulty Stone also acquired the rights to Jim Morrison's poetry.

The Doors was an ambitious project, considering that few films about rock and roll subjects had succeeded at the box office, apart from *La Bamba*, the story of Ritchie Valens, and the Gary Busey-starring biopic of Buddy Holly (in whose plane death crash Valens, ironically, had died as well). It was also another very different film for Oliver Stone to make.

Although the film was called *The Doors*, it was really about Jim Morrison. Stone talked to over 40 witnesses of Morrison's life. Everyone had a different story.

It's like *Citizen Kane*. I could have made a movie just talking to the witnesses. So I chose the other route, where the central character confides in the camera and says what's on his mind. There is still a mystery, but the relationship to the camera is very frontal. He's not hiding. His innermost thoughts are coming out with the poems and songs.

The film begins with Morrison, played by Val Kilmer, reciting his poem 'The Movie' in a voice-over:

The movie will begin in five moments
The mindless voice announced
All those unseated will await the next show
We filed slowly, languidly into the hall
The auditorium was vast and silent
As we seated and were darkened, the voice continued
The program for this evening is not new
You've seen the entertainment through and through
You've seen your birth, your life and death
You might recall all the rest
Did you have a good world when you died?
Enough to base a movie on?

In the New Mexico desert in 1949 the Morrison family drives past the wrecked truck of a group of Navajo Indians. As the young Jim Morrison, played by Sean Stone, watches this death scene, he hears his mother's words: 'It's only a dream, Jimmy.'

Then at UCLA film school Morrison's work is dismissed by his fellow students as pretentious, and as 'a little incoherent' by his teacher – who is played by Stone himself. Morrison announces that he is quitting the course.

The story of *The Doors* was essentially that of the rise of the group and Morrison's miserable death in Paris from a heroin overdose. After Janis Joplin and Jimi Hendrix died, Morrison would announce to whoever was listening, 'You're drinking with number three.'

I would like to believe that he went out smiling [Stone told *Rolling Stone*]. He liked it; he enjoyed it as it happened because he was in love with the death experience. He wanted to experience it, and he did. He had busted the limits on sex, for himself; on drugs, he'd taken every kind of drug; on the law, he busted the law, which I think hurt him the most, the trial really beat him down and tired him out, made him more aware of orthodoxy and the inevitable triumph of orthodoxy; and I think he busted through on the concept of success. He had success, he was God on earth for a while, he had everything he wanted, and he got bored with it. I think he became enamoured of failure. He went on a failure trip, too, and I think he enjoyed busting through on the failure trip by making a fool of himself in public, many times. He wanted to be an asshole; he wanted to be hated.

The film is set amidst numerous archetypal scenarios that present an alternative version of the much mythologized Sixties to that experienced by Ron Kovic – or by Oliver Stone, as he then was. Some of these are generalized, of the era: the youth riot on Sunset Strip in Los Angeles in 1967; the Summer of Love the same year in San Francisco; Andy

Warhol's pop subculture in New York; and a montage of quintessential television images: Kent State, Charles Manson, the moon landing, Martin Luther King, My Lai, Robert Kennedy, Nixon, Vietnam. Others are specifically related to Jim Morrison, and often involve the forces of law and order: Morrison maced in a shower stall in New Haven in 1968; his arrest and subsequent trial for simulating masturbation during a show in Miami in 1969.

Morrison's love of excess and his arrogance take quantum leaps: he voraciously consumes women, drugs, and alcohol. Despite his multitudinous dalliances, however, Morrison sticks with the somewhat monstrous Pamela (Meg Ryan) until the end. Yet, as Ron Kovic had also permanently experienced, Morrison suffers from a frequent lack of potency.

In a pivotal witchcraft scene Morrison drinks blood, snorts coke, and has sex with reporter Patricia Kennealy (Kathleen Quinlan); but as a counterbalance to this, the film swings around a less dark version of Morrison's metaphysical quest in a trip sequence involving Navajo Indians and desert peyote visions. This ends with a close-up of an old Indian warrior's eye in which we see a flash-forward shot of Morrison dead in a Paris bathtub.

In one scene Morrison is onstage when suddenly Native American shamans are dancing with him. This came from a story that Ray Manzarek had told Stone, of how the singer would emit a screech and Manzarek would think, 'This is not the soul of a white man, there's an Indian in there.'

The form of the movie was strongly influenced by the journey aspect of Fellini's *La Dolce Vita* as well as Bob Fosse's *All That Jazz*, a state-of-the-art film in dealing with the concept of non-linear time: Stone's impressionistic, semi-stream-of-consciousness film was to be structured around the music of the Doors and Jim Morrison's poetry.

For his lead character, the director chose Val Kilmer, mainly known at the time for his part in the not undistinguished epic *Willow*. There was an irony in this, for Kilmer had also played opposite Tom Cruise as his rival in *Top Gun*: and during the making of *Born on the Fourth of July*, Oliver Stone had observed the distance that Tom Cruise seemed to feel he needed to put around himself. Wasn't this someone who knew rock star-like pressures, who was young and under enormous strain, unable to walk down the street without being approached by a fan? 'And I used some of that in *The Doors* – it helped me understand what it was like to be Jim, surrounded by women and autograph-seekers and everybody wanting you.'

Like some kind of shamanic powerhouse, Stone endlessly worried away at Val Kilmer, insisting on more and more music rehearsals. He would even send over doctors with vitamin shots for him, to try to get him

Oliver Stone filming The Doors.

up to the strong physical level of Morrison. Appropriately for an actor playing a young rock star, Kilmer himself pushed Stone into a paternal role, as though he was a musician's manager. And when he observed a deep rebellious streak within Kilmer ('If you tell him something, he'll baa like a sheep.'), Stone realized he'd picked the right man for the job.

This became doubly apparent when Kilmer recorded the vocals for the film – a non-smoker, he devoured True Blues to coarsen his voice – and members of the original group thought they had been sung by Morrison. Val Kilmer, meanwhile, announced that he considered Stone's approach to his subject to be 'tits and acid'.

With *Born on the Fourth of July* it seemed that Stone had mastered the art of making epic films at a reasonable cost. The logistics of *The Doors* were enormous, however, and at $38 million it was Oliver Stone's most expensive film to date – it went $6 million over budget. The film used a total of 80 locations and 32,000 extras. For the filming of the Miami concert alone, they employed over 3,000 extras. Some of the stage performances, on which there would be five or six cameras, were as complicated to shoot as the battle scenes in *Platoon* or *Born on the Fourth of July*.

> The camera tries to share the exhilaration and the madness and the freedom – it's a totally free camera [said Stone]. I always respected the camera as another actor. I hate the type of direction that makes the camera a slave. I always respect the camera. I walk on the set...and I see the actor, I see the camera, and I see myself. I see a triangle. So that the camera...is as much a human participant as I am. It's an interesting relationship. So often the camera will speak to me on the day and say: 'No, this. That.' And it will become clear to me. So I might sit here and for days make notes on what I want to do, as I would with an actor.

Shooting took 60 days, the longest filming schedule yet for an Oliver Stone picture. It was not without its tensions: Val Kilmer started to 'method out' on his role, becoming increasingly anguished at getting into Morrison's death-trip state of mind and, as a consequence, he and Stone had their difficult moments; filming on Sunset Boulevard was expensive, a logistical nightmare, and psychically draining, as it felt as though Oliver Stone was under the judgemental microscope of the entire Hollywood film industry. After filming a Morrison trip sequence in the Californian Mitchell Caverns, paint powder became sucked into the walls – the film equipment was seized by the park authorities until the paint had been cleaned off. There were lighter moments, however, such as when Stone and his friend Richard Rutowski borrowed the Warner Brothers company jet and flew off to South Dakota for a weekend peyote

Val Kilmer and Oliver Stone making The Doors. **Kilmer became so immersed in his character that he began seriously to 'method out'.**

session with Native Americans that was justified as 'research'.

Before the film was released, another problem surfaced. Keyboard player Ray Manzarek, who is played in the film by Kyle MacLachlan, was widely viewed as the second most important member of the group after Morrison. For reasons of his own, he took serious umbrage with Stone's interpretation of the history of the group. Because of this 'Ray Manzarek faction', says Stone, 'people were taking camps before the movie was even finished. I tell you, so many people were just: I'm gonna hate this movie. It was awful. So that by the time it came out it wasn't even looked at as unto itself.'

Considering the cultural quicksand into which he had stepped – not only was Stone teetering on the verge of critical unfashionability, but Jim Morrison was considered by some to have been pretentious and puerile – The Doors had reasonable reviews. In the New York Times Janet Maslin caught this dichotomy, writing of the 'love-hate reaction' that the group inspired. 'Mr Stone,' she wrote, 'retains his ability to grab an audience by the throat and not let go; and retain that hold for hours; and he's succeeded in raising the dead.' Maslin's review pretty much matched the general tone – which was partially one of surprise that Stone had managed to pull it off. In the Village Voice, for example, J. Hoberman wrote: 'Against all odds, the stage performances are actually the movie's most compelling scenes.'

Partially, however, it seemed that critics didn't quite know what to make of the film. In fact, the distanced aspect of many reviews approximated an aspect of the movie: that The Doors can seem all exterior, lacking an inner dynamic and perception – especially when compared to the great insights and subjectivity in an admittedly very different film such as Platoon.

Although it did good business when it opened, box-office receipts soon tailed off. With foreign sales and video rights, however, this marginal epic easily made back its money.

9 JFK

At the beginning of May 1990, two months after the release of *The Doors*, Oliver Stone was presented with the eighth annual Upton Sinclair Award by the Liberty Hill Foundation, a Southern California fund-raising source for 'change-oriented, grassroots organizations.'

At a testimonial dinner in Beverly Hills, Michael Douglas described Stone's films as 'part craft, part crackle and part residual rage, which is a dynamic reflection of Oliver's own personality – broiling action, hyperactive camera movement, rapid exchanges, characters in excessive situations who behave in excessive ways, but have a sort of innocence of men to whom moral choices are still part of their landscape.'

Ron Kovic, meanwhile, told Stone he would be remembered 'many generations from now because of your courage, because you are not afraid to tell the truth.'

Speaking of what he was felt was the collective responsibility of Hollywood, Oliver Stone stated that it could 'take people further into oblivion or we can move and motivate, make people think and question. We are a formidable force, and it is essential that we use that power responsibly.'

He loved making movies, the director affirmed. 'It is my passion and my life, and I bury myself in it. I have been able to address some important issues – politically and personally. I hope my movies have made people think. I know they've angered a lot, been awarded by some, and have been avoided by many.'

But such responses as his films had already received were nothing compared with those awaiting Oliver Stone as he embarked on his most controversial movie to date. In two of the interviews that he did for *The Doors*, he had given clues as to the subject of his next film. To *Rolling Stone*, he had described his return to the United States after Vietnam:

I took the bus all the way down through Oregon, California, talking to guys in bus stations and cheap hotels. And trying to get laid with hookers in Oakland. I met a lot of Lee Harveys. I met a lot of guys who were really screwed up. The drifter mentality in American society is very interesting. But Oswald is a lot deeper than everybody thinks he is. He wasn't just a drifter; he was something else, too.

And in *US* magazine he had come right out with it:

I don't set out to make movies about big, controversial themes. I just make movies about what has happened to my life. ...My next movie's about the Kennedy assassination, which was the turning-point of my whole generation. Loss of innocence. Loss of security. The world started to seem dark and crazy. It's funny. I have to keep digging into our history to understand what happened to me and my generation.

This story of the assassination of President John F. Kennedy, the 35th President of the United States, in Dealey Plaza, Dallas, Texas, on 22 November 1963, was a pivotal moment in the history of the twentieth century.

Where had Oliver Stone been when it happened? In his room during lunch break at the Hill School in Pennsylvania; a fellow student ran in and said, 'They just shot the President.' At the time, still influenced by his father's politics and long before his subsequent radicalization, Stone was a Republican. All the same, as he told *Time*,

It was shocking to me because Kennedy was a handsome young man. I loved his rhetoric. Politically, I was against him because I was for Nixon and Goldwater. But in my heart I could not help being moved by his charisma. It was very sad for the family. We watched TV the whole weekend, just like in the movie. Then we moved on with our lives. We didn't really think about it. That was the point.

At first almost everyone around the world seemed to accept that Kennedy had been killed by 'lone nut' Lee Harvey Oswald, firing from the sixth floor of the Texas School Book Depository. That he left a trail of clues, including killing police officer Tippit, that led to him being arrested in a cinema shortly afterwards seemed to fit the character of the rather stupid, feckless follower of Fidel Castro that he was portrayed as being. That local nightclub owner Jack Ruby managed to gun him down in front of the TV cameras inside Dallas police station didn't even seem especially untoward – as the killing of the President indicated, that was clearly how they did things down there. The Warren Commission studied all the facts and duly delivered its verdict: Lee Harvey Oswald killed President John F. Kennedy. Case closed.

Over the years, however, you started to notice that strange deaths seemed to occur to a disproportionate number of people on the fringes of

Oliver Stone shooting a major JFK **crowd sequence.**

the case. Ruby's links to the Mob were made clear – at one point he had even worked for Al Capone. Oswald, meanwhile, was shown to have emigrated to the Soviet Union, and closer examination suggested that during this entire extremely odd phase of his life he could have been working for the CIA all along.

By the early 1970s an entire 'conspiracy theory' industry had sprung up around the assassination of Kennedy. In this the 'Zapruder film', an 8mm home movie of Kennedy being hit by bullets as he travelled in the motorcade, played a central part, as did mysterious figures moving behind the 'grassy knoll' that overlooked the plaza. Whilst you became aware that one person's conspiracy was another's group of like-minded friends, it seemed incontestable that Lee Harvey Oswald had not been alone in shooting Kennedy – if he did it at all; and the murder seemed to have been the work of a cabal of Cuban exiles, the Mafia, right-wing Southerners, and possibly the CIA. Did anyone believe any longer in the findings of the Warren Commission? Apparently not: a poll conducted before *JFK* was released found that 77 per cent of Americans doubted its findings and believed there had been a conspiracy. The only people in the United States who still seemed to accept it, as Oliver Stone was soon to find, were those in positions of Establishment power.

It's ridiculous to be demeaned as a conspiracy theorist – as a joke [he said to me]. To be equated with Elvis-Is-Alive people. It's just so demeaning and ridiculous, because anyone who looks at this logically...if there weren't some doubts in their mind about this thing, they really need a brain. There's just so much evidence against the lone nut.

It's so bizarre to have two weird things happen, much less the autopsy, much less the history of Lee Harvey Oswald, much less the history of Jack Ruby, much less the behaviour of certain people on that day. To defend that is so ridiculous.

1988 had seen the publication of *On the Trail of the Assassins*, a book by Jim Garrison, the former district attorney of New Orleans, now a Louisiana Appellate Court Justice. Between 1967 and 1969 Garrison had attempted to convict Clay Shaw, a right-wing local businessman, for conspiracy in the assassination of John F. Kennedy. Garrison had learned of a drunken argument that had taken place between Jack Martin, a private detective, and Guy Bannister, a one-time member of the FBI who had known Lee Harvey Oswald: Oswald had spent the summer before Kennedy was killed handing out pro-Castro leaflets in New Orleans, and in 1964 a stack of these were discovered in Bannister's desk after he died. Garrison implicated other conspirators, including David Ferrie, a gay former Eastern Airlines pilot, who died of cancer before the case went to trial; and he pointed the finger at the involvement of more than a dozen specific groups – including the CIA, military industrialists, and anti- and pro-Cuban agitators. At his subsequent trial, Clay Shaw was found not guilty. Media and government forces, Garrison claimed, had constantly obstructed his case.

Oliver Stone read Garrison's book whilst working on *Born on the Fourth of July*; he decided to option it out of his own pocket for $250,000. (He often does this, shelling out money to prevent talk going around studios about projects he might be developing.) Meeting Garrison, he was impressed with what he saw as the man's integrity – how he had stuck to his point of view, even though his personal life had collapsed around him as a consequence, a position the director understood well. Stone also took out an option on another book about the Kennedy killing, *Crossfire: The Plot That Killed Kennedy* by Jim Marrs. Then he devoured every volume available about the murder. Researchers were hired, and he engaged Zachary Sklar, who had edited Garrison's book, as co-writer. Personally undertaking his own sequence of interviews, Stone flew to Washington DC to talk to Colonel L. Fletcher Prouty, the Mr X character in the movie who is played by Donald Sutherland. 'It was one of the most extraordinary afternoons I've ever spent. Pretty much like in the movie, he just started to talk. And when he started to talk it sounded sure truthful to me: it came out like that and it hit me like that.'

Colonel Prouty described to Oliver Stone how at the time of the Kennedy killing he had been mysteriously sent to the South Pole as military escort for a group of VIPs. In a voice-over sequence in the subsequent film, Prouty's information is delivered by Sutherland to Jim Garrison:

It wasn't until I was on my way back in New Zealand that I read of the President's murder. Now, Oswald was charged at 7 p.m. Dallas time with Tippit's murder. That was 2 in the afternoon the next day New Zealand time, but already the paper had the entire history of an unknown 24-year-old man, Oswald – a studio picture, detailed biographical dates, Russian information – and were pretty sure of the fact he'd killed the President alone, although it took them four more hours to charge him with the murder in Texas.

Specifically, Prouty wondered one thing: why had he been sent to the South Pole when it would otherwise have been his task to have arranged for additional security in Dallas on 22 November that year? Security, he told Stone, had been abysmal. Without question he would have put between 100 and 200 agents on the sidewalks: the previous month in the same city UN Ambassador Adlai Stevenson had been spat upon. As his character says in *JFK*: 'Never would've allowed that limousine to slow down to 10 miles an hour, much less take that unusual curve at Houston and Elm. You would have felt an Army presence in the streets that day, but none of this happened. It was a violation of the most basic protection codes we have. And it's the best indication of a massive plot in Dallas.'

Strange things were afoot that day, Prouty told Stone, who put the details straight into his script. The entire Cabinet was out of the way on a trip to the Far East; a third of a combat division – a handy amount for riot control – was in the air above the United States, returning from Germany; at 12.34, three minutes after the shooting, the entire telephone system in Washington DC went dead for one hour (in fact, the system didn't go out altogether and only behaved erratically); word was radioed from the White House Situation Room to Lyndon Johnson that one individual had been Kennedy's killer.

Prouty, said Stone, was 'a key guy. He told me the story of what he believed and he just blew my socks off. Very much like he did Costner in the movie.'

> And I just sat there. 'What the fuck am I going to do about this? What the fuck am I going to do about this?' I'm just a useless lone individual against state power. And once you go against state power – whatever country in the world you're in – you're in for a rough ride. Russia, Peru, China… Here's no different. And I have. I've challenged it. I've ridiculed it. And I've attacked it. And I'm still attacking it. But it's not my only mission in life. It's just something I feel strongly about: the rights of the individual to think for himself and to be free.

Like his two previous films, *JFK* had an epic scope. But it also had a multiplicity of parallel plots. To accommodate these, Oliver Stone wrote the film very much from an impressionistic point of view. 'Zak [Sklar], who was the editor for Jim Garrison's books, gave me most of the information. But essentially it's my structure. And the structure was fragmented.'

The decision to yet again take an almost stream-of-consciousness approach was, says Stone, 'based slightly on a false premise'. Although he did employ ideas from Kurosawa's *Rashomon*, with its kaleidoscope of viewpoints, his principal model was the Constantin Costa-Gavras political thriller *Z*.

> And I had an erroneous impression of its structure. Somehow I had the impression that in Z you had the showing of the crime and then the re-showing of the crime through the picture until it was seen in another way. That was the idea of *JFK* – that was the essence of it: basically, that's why I called it *JFK*. Not J dot F dot K dot. *JFK*. It was a code, like Z was a code, for he lives, American-style. As it was written it became more fascinating: it evolved into four DNA threads.
>
> There are four structures there: The Garrison story from the centre was very good up through the New Orleans section, but essentially was a smaller story

Stone considered Kevin Costner to carry the same All American frontier qualities as James Stewart: so he was ideal to play the pivotal role in JFK **of Jim Garrison, the New Orleans district attorney.**

about a man following a local lead to its natural conclusion – he couldn't get any further than that.

And the second story that evolved from the research was the fascination of the Oswald legend: who he was and how to try to inculcate that.

Then the third idea was to go to Dealey Plaza and recreate the murder, and then see it again and again through the movie. Because Jim never went to Dealey Plaza: he goes once in the book. That was never his domain: his domain was the New Orleans territory. How do you get the New Orleans story combined with the Texas story? That was a very tricky thing. So that was the idea to go parallel.

And during this research the fourth thing happened to me which was that through contacts I was introduced to and approached Colonel Fletcher Prouty.

That became the fourth story. It became the means by which we were able to move between New Orleans, local, into the wider national story of Dealey Plaza. The trial within the movie has national implications, but in reality the trial was just a local, little affair. For example, I don't believe that at the trial Jim Garrison ever went through an exhibition of Dealey Plaza like we did. I wanted to show it with models. I don't think he ever did that. I think his case was based on the few witnesses he had against Shaw.

To hold the audience's interest throughout this complex plot, Oliver Stone opted for the same approach that had been taken in the Second World War epic about D-Day, *The Longest Day*: he filled the film with star names. Kevin Costner played Jim Garrison, with Sissy Spacek as his wife. Lee Harvey Oswald was tackled by Gary Oldman with his habitual psychotic flair – he spent time with Marina, Oswald's wife, and with his two daughters; Tommy Lee Jones played Clay Shaw, the gay ex-CIA operative – he was nominated for an Academy Award as Best Supporting Actor; Joe Pesci was almost surreal as David Ferrie; Ed Asner, the liberal activist, played former FBI agent Guy Banister; Jack Lemmon and Walter Matthau brought their cinematic weight to bear, as of course did Donald Sutherland as X. Several of these seasoned pros were extremely impressed by the speedy professionalism with which Stone worked.

The Jim Garrison sequences of *JFK* used New Orleans as their location. Yet Oliver Stone was by now used to shooting in Texas, so it was clearly useful that much of the film was set there. Why, now he could even shoot in Dealey Plaza, filming from the same sixth-floor window from which Oswald supposedly fired, undermining years of public relations campaigns to prevent the city being perceived as a place where they shoot presidents.

On the first day of filming in Dealey Plaza, as between 50 and 60 extras sat around at the front of the Book Depository, a large pane of sheet glass fell straight down from the sixth floor. Kevin Costner watched aghast as it hurtled downwards like a guillotine blade towards the extras. At the last moment a gust of wind caught it and moved it away from them to where it smashed to the ground without causing any injuries. In this moment Costner felt that any negative energy that had been trying to prevent the film had been irrevocably dispersed. For a moment, he caught Oliver Stone's eye. Stone nodded and carried on with his task of directing the movie.

The filming was an enormous physical challenge in itself. The script was 156 pages long; and in order to carry the four interlocking plots, it was extremely complex. The shoot was only scheduled for 79 days, however, in the middle of the summer of 1991: the budget from Warner Brothers was $40 million.

Much of the time Bob Richardson was also shooting neo-documentary footage and black-and-white video sequences of the same scenes. At Richardson's suggestion Stone let his DP shoot the first section of the Dealey Plaza sequence in 16mm, mostly in black-and-white. In his darker moments Oliver Stone wondered whether this would be his *Heaven's Gate*.

His anxiety increased when *Washington Post* national security correspondent George Lardner turned up on the set uninvited. Stone was worried: he knew of Lardner's many CIA connections and suspected an attempt at disinformation. With reason: Lardner wrote a 5,000-word piece in the *Post* that carried the headline: 'On the Set: Dallas in Wonderland.' The subtitle even more fully revealed the article's intent: 'How Oliver Stone's Version of the Kennedy Assassination Exploits the Edge of Paranoia'.

Somehow Lardner had obtained a first draft of the script and spent his sizeable editorial space picking holes in it. Pointedly, he also suggested that Garrison had focused on Clay Shaw's homosexual relations to boost his case. Shaw and many of his associates were gay. Oliver Stone, already under the scrutiny of the guardians of Establishment thinking, now also found himself having to assure the gay community that there was nothing homophobic in the film.

Lardner's piece troubled Stone. It looked as though the Kennedy conspiracy theory Black Hole was opening up again, possibly to swallow him.

Filming of *JFK* ended only five short months before the film was due to have its Christmas opening.

The task of editing the film looked formidable. *JFK* had 200 speaking parts and 2,000 'visual effect' opticals – a colossal amount. There were also real archival and restaged historical images. The final film had some 2,800 shots.

But Oliver Stone turned this adversity to advantage, and in the process revolutionized the form of film structure. From *JFK* onwards a fundamental shift took place in the construction of his films. This approach had been dabbled with in *The Doors*, but was firmly written into the script of *JFK* as part of its form: in essence the film uses a simple detective story structure; yet *JFK* doesn't offer an omniscient point of view; there is a much more subjective, lateral presentation of the plot, the rhythm of the editing carrying the story.

For *JFK* Oliver Stone brought in Hank Corwin, a highly respected commercials editor. Stone chose him specifically because his 'highly chaotic mind' was 'totally alien to the film form'.

He was an associate on *JFK* and he irritated some of the more traditional editors – I remember the conflict. Hank's concepts are very commercial – sixty-seconds-get-your-attention-fragment-your-mind-make-you-rethink-it. But he had not developed the long form yet. And so a lot of his cuts were very chaotic.

There were further problems. *JFK* was the last film cut by Oliver Stone before he moved on to the new technology of digital editing. To try and move ahead more swiftly, much of the film's footage was transferred to tape for editing. A minor nightmare developed: time codes disappeared, leaving no way to keep track of the sound-cutting.

Against all the odds, however, *JFK* was completed and ready for its 20 December release in the USA. Warners had backed the film with a $15 million publicity campaign. At the same time as this kicked in, however, there was a fierce counter-attack from the Establishment media. In the *New York Times* a story ran under the headline 'Does *JFK* Conspire Against Reason?'; the *Washington Post* ran a further piece against the film: 'Kennedy Assassination: How About The Truth?' by former President Gerald Ford, a member of the Warren Commission; in the *Wall Street Journal* there was an article entitled 'A Better Conspiracy Than Oliver Stone's'; and in the first week that *JFK* was in the cinemas, it made the cover of *Newsweek*, but with the strap-line 'Why Oliver Stone's new movie can't be trusted'.

For the next month there were articles everywhere damning the film, pounding the director with negative press. And threats to Oliver Stone's life were made to his office. He countered with a publicity campaign in both political and populist arenas: Oliver Stone was omnipresent, from Dan Rather's CBS Evening News show to 'Oprah Winfrey'.

And he succeeded. Today it is difficult to fool a media-aware public. They can taste the rot when officialdom attempts to push its thinking on to them. By the end of January 1992 *JFK* had taken in over $50 million at the box office: the film was already just about in profit.

Stone's conclusion in *JFK* had been that the assassination was a military coup prompted by – among other things – Kennedy's desire to begin disengaging US troops from Vietnam. It doesn't really matter whether you agree with the particular details of Oliver Stone's version of the conspiracy: whether you think that the Bay of Pigs Cubans or southern Rightists or the Mafia had more or less importance in the global scheme than the military or the CIA or any other bunch of self-righteous loonies who have been missed out. The fact is, all the elements are there for you, up on the screen. Take your pick and choose your assassins: these blinkered men kill Presidents and peasants.

10 Heaven and Earth

As an infantryman in Vietnam, Oliver Stone had been distrustful of all Vietnamese – they posed a threat to him and his friends. Later Stone gained a greater awareness: that the GIs and Vietnamese civilians had a common bond – 'fear and the need to survive under any circumstances'.

But he came to see that his films had helped create some imbalance in the perception of the war. '*Platoon* and *Born on the Fourth of July* told specific, grunt's-eye-view stories of the hellish misery our foot soldiers went through in that far-off place,' he wrote in the introduction to a book about his next film, *Heaven and Earth*.

> What's been missing from the screen is the reverse angle on the Vietnamese: what the war – or wars – were like from the perspective of the people living in Vietnam, a country with more than a thousand rich years of history and culture. And more particularly, what were the experiences of the innocent peasant farmers, interested in little more than their seasonal plantings and harvestings, their families and kin, having enough to eat from month to month, praying to the Buddha and their ancestors? These hard-working souls, with one eye on the heaven above them and the other on the earth that brought forth sustenance and regenerative life, were the wars' most tragic victims.

The director had discovered the personification of the Vietnamese experience in Le Ly Hayslip, who had told her story in two powerful autobiographies, *When Heaven and Earth Changed Places* and *Child of War, Woman of Peace*.

> Buddhist spirituality, reverence for ancestors, and respect for the land were three of the strongest elements of Le Ly's story that attracted my interest [said Stone]. None of these themes had yet been approached in a film about Vietnam, and I was eager to explore them dramatically and visually...
>
> There were names and faces and histories attached to those bodies littering one end of Vietnam to the other between 1963 and 1975. *Heaven and Earth* is the story of just one family, and as Le Ly constantly and generously reminds me, many others suffered even more than the Phungs.

> When I first began talking to Oliver about his screenplay [noticed Le Ly Hayslip]
> he showed a father's concern not just for the health and appearance of his new
> offspring, but for its spirit, too. He knew no story about the Vietnamese could
> be complete if he showed only our beautiful land and handsome people and
> all the suffering we'd been through. To tell the whole story, he must also explore
> the world inside.
>
> ...Soul, I believe, is what Oliver's movies are all about. He told me he makes
> his films the way a father raises a child: doing the best he can to nurture it and
> make it strong – to give it a sense of humanity and its own life force – then
> letting it go to find its own way in the world.

Attempting to simply get on with their lives in the Central Vietnamese
village of Ky La, Le Ly Hayslip's family had tried to ignore the coercions
of both the South Vietnamese and the Viet Cong. Eventually, however, the
corruption of the ruling regime and their American allies led to her brothers joining the North Vietnamese; Le Ly herself spied for the Viet Cong.

When she was arrested and tortured by government troops, she was
saved by her brother-in-law's political influence. But then she was
perceived as a traitor by the Viet Cong, and raped by two of their soldiers.
Moving to Saigon with her mother, they took a job as domestic help. Her
employer soon got her pregnant, however, and his wife fired her. Living
the life of a street hustler, Le Ly sold black market goods until she met a
55-year-old American contractor, transmogrified in the film to a US
sergeant ten years younger, who fell in love with her.

With the fall of Saigon, she agreed to marry him and was evacuated to
the United States with her child. There she found herself involved in a
new internal struggle as she fought to understand this new bungalow
ranch-style life and culture that included the difficulty of being part of a
multi-racial couple. Eventually her husband committed suicide.
Attempting to make sense of her endlessly traumatic life and perceive its
universal message, Le Ly Hayslip started the East Meets West
Foundation and medical institutions in Central Vietnam.

> Spirit life, as opposed to physical life, is evident in all our efforts to unify
> ourselves in our life [said Oliver Stone]. I think it's the case in most of my movies
> that whatever pressure is brought to bear on an individual, he is made aware
> in some way so that he brings out the enlightenment inside, grows from it hope-
> fully, becomes another person, and his being changes in the course of the movie.
> Not only his physical wellbeing, but also his spiritual and mental wellbeing.
>
> *Heaven and Earth* is deliberately structured that way. As a religious journey,
> as a spiritual journey. There's a woman who regards all the obstacles of her life
> in an interesting way, as a means by which she can challenge herself to
> enlighten herself, to grow as a person. Not to strike out in revenge, not to seek

vengeance, but to seek feeling good. She looks at suffering as a tool. That was perhaps the film in which I had the first conscious awareness of having done that deliberately. And that is Buddhism. I think in that film I was prone to see all experience as positive. More so than in previous films. Does that make sense?

Making *Heaven and Earth* brought about profound changes for the director. For example, Oliver Stone began to re-explore Buddhism, which he had first encountered in Vietnam, turning the backyard treehouse at his Santa Monica home into a shrine. He arranged for monks, who arrived in saffron robes, to bless the film. 'I guess Le Ly Hayslip being Buddhist finally convinced me this was the direction to go, and I crossed gradually. My friend Richard Rutowski had been into it for 25 years. He was very helpful. We went to Tibet and India and it just flowed – it came about.'

Of course, not only would Oliver Stone's third film about the Vietnamese war give the point of view of an inhabitant of the invaded country, but that person would be female – a charge constantly levelled at the director by his detractors was that Oliver Stone's world was so macho that he was unable to write strong female characters.

It was about a woman, the Yin side, that bizarrely complemented my yang side [he told me]. In some ways, I am the Tommy Lee Jones character in the movie. He is the American figure that is heroic over there, and in America he ends up being the one who can't cope with American life. And she as the immigrant does better. There seemed to be a brutal irony in that. He's like the end of the tradition. He cannot change or be flexible. She is flexible. She has been taught flexibility by life. Not just by being a woman but because it's her nature. She is the adapted gene. She is able to go on. His is the rigid gene. There's an absolutist quality about the Tommy Lee Jones character that cuts off, that is frightened and cannot go on.

There are more scenes, by the way, in that movie. I'm trying to make a director's cut. I had some scenes where she goes to see Father Bob, the Christian, played by Jeffrey Jones. She compares very innocently her native faith to Christianity. She wonders why there is this aggression, why violence is very much the visual schemata of the Christian church. Why the chief image is a man nailed to a cross. Why suffering is promoted and iconified like that. Which is a good question, because Buddhist images tend to be happier, more serene, and not about suffering. Suffering is a given, suffering is a part of life, but it's an illusion too. In Christian life, suffering is elevated to that of an icon.

Which make me think in our own films do we not put the emphasis on the sado-masochistic qualities in our own iconography – that we need to die for something, that we need to sacrifice for something. It cannot just be through enlightenment, which is undramatic. Which [laughs] is against film-making because I think film-making needs epiphanies that are violent or strong.

Oliver Stone in Thailand whilst filming Heaven and Earth**, a film that was one from the heart.**

In September 1991 Oliver Stone began casting the film. Tommy Lee Jones, who compared the *Heaven and Earth* screenplay to 'epic poetry', was cast as Sergeant Steve Butler; Joan Chen – who at one time had tried to option Hayslip's book to play her herself – was given the role of Le Ly's mother; Dr Hainh S. Ngor, who had won an Academy Award for his part in *The Killing Fields*, was to play her father, a part that required a make-up job that took almost three hours every morning; veteran Debbie Reynolds, who hadn't acted in a film for 20 years, was signed up as Abigail Butler, the sergeant's mother.

For the role of Le Ly Hayslip herself, however, Oliver Stone chose Hiep Thi Le, a 22-year-old physiology major at the University of California who had never acted before. Born in Vietnam, she had fled the country in 1979 as a 'boat person'.

On 19 October 1992 filming began on the Malay Peninsula in Thailand, where the village of Ky La had been created as it would have been in 1949. An eight-week shoot in Thailand was followed by a month's filming in Los Angeles for the American sequence of the film.

Before shooting started, Oliver Stone took Le Ly Hayslip on one side and informed her that her role was to be his 'technical adviser'. 'It will be just like going to war!' he said to her. 'Before we shoot a scene, you tell me if things look OK – the way you remember them or the way they used to be. After I say cut, you tell me how things turned out!'

> The assignment seemed simple enough [she thought]. But I soon learned that if I said, 'Oh, my father would have looked out the window before he said that – to see if anyone was listening,' or 'The MPs wouldn't have let those black-market girls so close to the compound,' he would call everyone back and re-shoot the scene. After a few of these episodes (and some irritated looks from the hard-working crew), I discovered the difference between comments that truly helped our 'offspring' to grow and those that merely stopped the show.

Hiep Thi Le noted 'the feelings of sadness that poured out of Oliver Stone, Le Ly, and the refugees... While there was action in front of the cameras, I noticed more what was happening behind the camera. The extras broke down like children in the midst of warfare! ...On the outside, a man like Oliver can appear to be tough and demanding, but inside he is as vulnerable and caring as the rest.'

The novice actress, however, was experiencing her own problems.

> At one point, I went into a state of seclusion due to the emotional trauma of having done the rape scene. I had constant nightmares, I was afraid to look at or speak to anyone because I thought I might bring them into my sleep. I remember Oliver coming into my trailer to try and speak to me. He was not successful and was hurt like the others. But he did not give up.

Clearly *Heaven and Earth* was one from the heart for Oliver Stone, part of his sense of responsibility toward the Vietnamese people. The film was considered the final third of Stone's 'Vietnam Trilogy'. But, he said, 'I could make 20 more films about the war, so great a role did it play in my life and the soul of our country and the world.'

Vietnamese refugees living in camps in Thailand were used in their hundreds as extras, and the scenes were often as emotional for them.

> We are so happy to see this movie being made [said a 70-year-old man who had been brought up in the next village to Le Ly Hayslip's Ky La]. People working here from all over the world are using their hearts, minds, bodies, and physical strength, day and night, to tell our story. This is a movie for the whole world to see and understand. We are refugees from the wars. We take refuge in all parts of the world. We are in Thailand. Some of our new friends are in America. We are everywhere except our home...Vietnam.

The irony, poetry even, of *Heaven and Earth* being the first film Stone had made with a woman as the lead character would be compounded by the problems that were about to arise with the woman with whom he had been sharing his life since 1981, Elizabeth Stone. In fact, a great strain was already being felt by the director during the course of the actual filming.

On 13 October 1991, Michael Jack Stone had been born, a brother to Sean. The birth of a child can often complicate a relationship. Problems from the parents' own childhoods can be brought out as a consequence. The first couple of years of a new child's life are a tricky time for any man-woman partnership. The closest of couples can sometimes split up as their nerve-endings are inextricably raked with pain from their own pasts. And Oliver and Elizabeth Stone had not had the easiest of relationships.

Stone almost seemed to have made a virtue of his indiscretions, for which he was as legendary in Hollywood as for his interest in the effects of hallucinogenics. Of late he had become especially interested in ayahuasca, the legendary tea made from an infusion of Brazilian jungle vines: its Castaneda-like qualities appealed to someone who named his production company Ixtlan before the name was altered to Illusion Entertainment. (Having become co-producer with Ed Pressman of *Reversal of Fortune*, for which Jeremy Irons won the Academy Award for Best Actor in 1991, Oliver Stone now had three other films in development: *South Central*, *Zebrahead*, and *Joy Luck Club*.)

Not long after *JFK* had come out Stone had travelled down to Brazil to experience ayahuasca with Richard Rutowski, his friend and fellow traveller in the psychedelic quest. An extremely powerful hallucinogenic, of which DMT is the principal constituent part, ayahuasca takes you on a journey that seems never to fail to reveal what your soul wants you to know at that specific time: as a consequence, it can sometimes be a rollercoaster ride through your psyche in which you visit both heaven and hell – or it can be a mild, blissful experience of great contentment in which, for example, you travel back to a rather earlier existence as an amoeba on the sea-bed.

At this stage no doubt Oliver Stone might rather have been an amoeba on a sea-bed. Elizabeth Stone had seemed to be the only person in Oliver's world who was unaware that he led a constant double life. Although she had discovered he had been having an affair during the making of *Wall Street*, their marriage had managed to weather this storm. When she found his diary, however, shortly after he had left to begin filming *Heaven and Earth* in Thailand, she discovered the truth about her husband's other life.

She telephoned him in Thailand and announced she was filing for divorce. Stone asked her to come out to join him on the set, and there was something of a reconciliation. When filming moved to the United States, they continued to live together in the family home. However, it was the beginning of the end of their marriage.

> That was an important film. It changed my life. People who know my work don't realize how important it was to me. A divorce occurred there, a whole change in my life pattern. I put an end to the old way of living. I gave up my children in a sense to do that, and went on my own. Back to my earlier days of being free and outside the family structure. I've stayed very well with my kids, but honestly I did give up a way of life. Took another fork in the road.

Did he think he had benefited from this?

> Oh yes. Though who can say? My ex-wife would never agree. But I think I did. It's a whole new other Oliver. People tell me that I seem much happier than I've ever been in the last four or five years. They've seen a significant difference. Before I always seemed like I was busy. But I was under stress in a way, sort of fighting against my environment. I was very intense, but I didn't seem overall happy. That's what a lot of people tell me. Now I feel more like Kazantzakis. I made my life the way it is. I made it. I brought myself to this road. That's a great feeling of accomplishment. I'm here because I was what I once was. I'm not here because of falseness to myself. I'm doing the right thing, whatever it is. I am Zorba.
>
> But there are days when I think I must really be out of my fucking mind. [Laughs.] And a total failure, I suppose. In many ways. Those raindog days.

Heaven and Earth was the first Oliver Stone movie to be edited electronically: on a Lightworks, the British system. Hiep Thi Le had struggled valiantly in a role that had great range, and for the most part succeeded admirably. When contrasted with other more experienced actors, however, her inexperience showed, her performance sometimes seeming a little flat. When Tommy Lee Jones, a man at one of several peaks in his career, came on the screen, he simply took it over. You wanted to see more of him.

But the film had great heart, an acute sense of poetry, and an emotional intensity not felt in an Oliver Stone film since *Born on the Fourth of July*. Yet when it was released in December 1993, *Heaven and Earth* was critically trounced.

'Through this film,' Le Ly Hayslip had written in the book about the making of the movie,'...Americans will learn that introducing two cultures through the matchmaker of war was not the best path to compassion and understanding.'

Unfortunately, hardly any Americans saw the film. *Heaven and Earth* took in only six million dollars at the US box office. It was a great disappointment for Oliver Stone, and one that he feels to this day.

11 Natural Born Killers

At the end of the Eighties a prospective screenwriter called Roger Avary had written a script that he called *The End of the Road*. His friend and writing collaborator Quentin Tarantino re-wrote it until it was 400 pages long.

It told the story of a character called Clarence who writes a script about himself and his girlfriend Alabama whilst they are on the run, romanticizing themselves as the characters of Mickey and Malory Knox.

Roger Avary and Quentin Tarantino then stripped it down to what would become the foundations of the Tony Scott-directed film *True Romance* – it was Avary who wrote the first draft. Later Tarantino went back and fashioned what was left into what would become *Natural Born Killers*. He also pillaged parts of it for *Reservoir Dogs* and *Pulp Fiction*.

Shortly before Tarantino did a deal for *Reservoir Dogs*, it was optioned by Jane Hamsher and Don Murphy, a pair of former University of Southern California film majors who were struggling to set up a production company.

It was a good script [thought Hamsher]. I liked it a lot. It had a lot of energy to it. It was very much a Quentin script. It was very different from what we finally shot. It was just a romp. It didn't have any of the heavy moral overtones that Oliver laid on it. In fact, at the time it didn't have much of the characters of Mickey and Malory.

The two partners took the script to CB Pictures, who passed it on to Sean Penn. Penn in turn gave it to Thom Mount, the producer. 'Thom and Sean and Oliver Stone were sitting around at Oliver's house one night having dinner,' said Hamsher. 'Oliver asked Thom if he knew of any scripts he might be interested in making. So Oliver read *Natural Born Killers* and really liked it and asked if Sean was really attached. And Thom said no: he didn't think Sean had even read it.'

When Jane Hamsher and Don Murphy received a call from Oliver Stone's office asking them to come for a meeting with the director about

Natural Born Killers, their initial response was disbelief. 'We didn't believe it: we were nobodies. We thought it was full of shit,' she remembered.

But of course they went to the meeting at Stone's Santa Monica offices, with a measure of trepidation. 'I'd always thought in the press that he came across as a pompous bastard,' remembered Jane Hamsher. 'And I was struck when I met him that he didn't seem like that at all. He had a commanding presence, but he seemed very genuine and very sincere. And to this day I think Oliver's an extremely sincere person... But it depends on what he's on,' she laughs.

At the time Oliver Stone had just had a big hit with *JFK*, and was getting ready to shoot *Heaven and Earth*. 'He was a very confident Oliver. But he was extraordinarily paranoid about the press. I couldn't put Oliver and *Natural Born Killers* together, though: apart from *Talk Radio*, all his scripts had been original works. But he told us he wanted to confound his critics and just do something he wanted to do.'

Covering themselves, Don Murphy insisted that Oliver Stone had to agree to make *Natural Born Killers* as his next film after *Heaven and Earth* or they would take the project elsewhere. And the director agreed. 'Sometimes I thought it was kind of a midlife crisis and we were the new toy,' said Jane Hamsher.

'The Quentin script,' she continued, 'was very much Mickey and Malory as seen through the eyes of other people.' However, Stone said that whilst he was in Thailand shooting *Heaven and Earth*, he wanted Hamsher and Murphy to get someone they knew to re-work the script. They brought in Dave Veloz, a friend of theirs from USC, to do a rewrite for $5,000. 'So Dave wrote the first third of the movie. He wrote all of the Rodney Dangerfield stuff. He wrote all of the Mickey and Malory relationship stuff.'

There was a poetic synchronicity to such an approach. Whilst Oliver Stone was in Thailand, the rupture occurred in his own relationship with Elizabeth. 'So what he really wanted to concentrate on was the relationship between these two characters. A lot of the scenes were improvised and based on Oliver and Elizabeth's fights at the time.'

At first, Oliver Stone and his wife were trying to hold on to their marriage. Elizabeth even accompanied her husband on some of the location scouts for *Natural Born Killers*. Jane Hamsher noticed something of 'a strained atmosphere in pre-production'.

She also reacted with some surprise when Stone enthused over a particular setting as being 'ideal for my Indian scene'.

'Oliver,' she said, 'there isn't an Indian scene in the script.'

'Oh,' he replied, 'there's always one in my films.'

When Quentin Tarantino discovered that his script had been substantially rewritten, first by Don Veloz and then by Stone and Richard

Rutowski, he flipped. He declared war, first against Jane Hamsher and Don Murphy and then against Oliver Stone.

'He called up Oliver,' said Jane Hamsher, 'and said that he'd had actors read his script and Oliver's and they said Quentin's was better.'

Although initially he'd been taken by the sheer nihilism of the original Tarantino script, Oliver Stone had endeavoured to move *Natural Born Killers* up several levels. Reinforcing and expanding Tarantino's bleak vision, he and his co-writers had turned the screenplay into an acute satire on what he perceived as an expression of the television-induced torment of contemporary society – although there are those around Stone who believe such a philosophy about the movie was retrospective.

It was reputed to be this exploitation picture [he said], which is so far-fetched and away from what it actually is. The picture is a reflection of what we see. It is a form of vomiting up, absolutely – that's what I saw in the early Nineties. That sensationalism of television corrupting the culture for profit.

The whole thing was intended as a rollercoaster ride. The first half of the movie was designed as a wild ride; and the second half deliberately slows down to pick up its pace for the last riot: the prison slows you down. But the idea is that it is seething and then boils, boils, boils until it explodes. So that was the pace of the film: we had two acts, two different genres: road movie and prison movie.

They were two kids from the heartland. They were desensitized by what they had lived through. Not only by their families, but by television too. They are the Everyone who is victimized. They have just had enough, and they are exploding for their freedom.

And then they get smart in the second half: they start to understand the world. And they transcend the prison by using the media. Get rid of the media and fucking disappear. Their only solution is to disappear and get out of the system.

Shooting was scheduled to begin in May 1993, while the editing of *Heaven and Earth* was still being completed. Oliver Stone was also involved in his production work for Ixtlan at the same time. Such a work load was to some extent an escape for the director from his personal problems. But the actual making and content of *Natural Born Killers* was also a cathartic purging of elements of his psyche that had brought Oliver Stone to where he was at that point in his life.

Although Warner Brothers were nervous about the film, they agreed to back it so long as a big enough star would take the part of Mickey Knox. Although names like Mel Gibson and Kevin Costner were mentioned, Stone went for Woody Harrelson, the least well-known and bankable of the studio's suggestions. In this choice of leading man there was almost a psychic link to Stone's last cinema release, *JFK*: for Harrelson's father, who is serving a double life sentence for having shot to death a federal

Woody Harrelson might almost have been considered as born to play Mickey Knox in Natural Born Killers.

judge, has long been rumoured to have been one of the three men briefly arrested near the grassy knoll in Dallas from which Kennedy was probably killed. And Oliver Stone believed there was a genetic follow-through in Woody Harrelson – it was in his eyes, he insisted – that made him ideal to play Mickey Knox. As befitted someone who had started out in the TV sitcom *Cheers*, Harrelson also had a considerable sense of humour. Aware of Oliver Stone's disintegrating marriage – the director would occasionally make jokes about his impending divorce – Woody Harrelson threw in an acutely pointed ad lib near the end of the film. Wayne Gayle asks, 'So Mickey, when you get out of here, what do you want to do?' Mickey replies, 'I'm gonna get me a couple of Asian women and start that long healing process.'

For Mallory Knox, Stone picked Juliette Lewis 'I think Juliette fulfils that bill really well,' he said. 'She's that young, gawky, kind of teenage type. She's deadly, and has a heart at the same time. I liked her performance a lot.' For the part of Wayne Gale, the Australian TV newsman, Stone chose Robert Downey, Jr. 'Downey was great,' said Stone. 'He got it right away. Everyone did: Tom Sizemore, Robert, Juliette, Woody, Tommy Lee. They are all nuts – what a crazy bunch. There's not one sane person in the whole cast.'

Filming began on schedule in New Mexico in May 1993, on a sound stage in Albuquerque, and in Santa Fe, Winslow, Redrock, Taos, and the Shoshone and Navajo reservations. Although the first scenes shot were of footage that was to show on the screens for Wayne Gale's television show, the film was made roughly in chronological order. And at a frantic pace: Oliver Stone was insistent that filming be completed by 1 August. In the end *Natural Born Killers* turned into a 55-day shoot.

It was when filming moved to Stateville prison in Joliet, Illinois, however, that the action really hotted up.

> I really liked it there [said Jane Hamsher]. In fact, the only two people who really liked it were me and Oliver. Everyone else really hated it. I thought it was fascinating. I thought it was a really interesting place to be. I hate sets, and so does Oliver, by the way. I'm sure that's why he always wants to be on location, because it's the only thing that gets him going, gets him excited.

Stateville is a maximum security prison, with some 85 per cent of its inmates serving life terms. It has the largest perimeter wall of any prison in the United States, with a wall that extends eight feet into the earth to prevent prisoners tunnelling out. It was a tense place – there had been six executions there since 1990.

Oliver Stone had looked at other prisons, but none of them apart from Stateville had the requisitely claustrophobic *Riot in Cell Block 11* period feel for which he was searching. He made a deal with the prison authorities to install a $50,000 cable TV system as his fee for using the facility. Stone quickly made friends with 'Big Al', reputedly the second-in-command of one of the largest gangs in the United States, and the undisputed king of Stateville. When Oliver Stone had been to recce the prison months before the shoot he had visited the local county courthouse: a certain Raymond Sojack, a mild-mannered accountant who had murdered his wife and child, was on trial. Arriving at Stateville, Stone ran into Sojack. In the scene where Tommy Lee Jones grabs the black prisoner with the nose pliers, the bald white man looking on is Raymond Sojack.

The *Natural Born Killers* crew shot in the prison for two weeks. They set up tents outside the prison as a base camp, and hours would be lost every day as the crew cleared their equipment past the guards. Sometimes they didn't bring out as much as they took in: once a camera went missing.

Because of the chronological order they were following, the production then moved back to the sound stage. Returning to the prison, however, Stone discovered that he was unable to use some of the prisoners he'd first hired, who had been paid $25 a day. While he and his crew had been away, a major riot had broken out after members of one gang sold bad drugs to another gang. As a consequence two prisoners had died and eleven others had been hospitalized. In the ensuing riot some guards had been beaten up: the prison was now on lockdown. Not even 'Big Al' had any influence here.

Tensions were not confined to the prisoners. In the shot where Juliette Lewis runs into the prison door, Bob Richardson injured himself, breaking a finger, as Stone insisted he get closer and closer to the object. He and Oliver Stone were arguing with great frequency. But it was not only with his director that the DP was experiencing edginess. Richardson is known as a hard taskmaster who is rough on his crews. And undoubtedly their work environment took its toll on his work team: many of them were very nervous indeed during the jailbreak sequence, in which real prisoners were employed. 'His crew used to call him the billygoat, and they did not say it affectionately,' said Jane Hamsher. In fact, at the end of shooting the film they poured a bucket of ice water over him.

All the same, Richardson has fantastic energy; a grip confided how, whenever a new set of lights arrived, it would be Richardson who would be the first down unpacking them. 'Come on, come on! Let's go!'

You feel this energy in Richardson's work. In fact, in *Natural Born Killers* it is not just Bob Richardson's approach that is felt, but an entire work technique. For Richardson, who takes a hard political line, had initially told Oliver Stone that he didn't approve of the script and wouldn't be doing the job. 'You can't leave me now,' cried Stone. 'I've just lost my wife.' Stone had also parted company before the film with his long-time producer Alex Ho.

Bob Richardson agreed to be director of photography on *Natural Born Killers* if he could use whatever techniques he deemed necessary. Trusting the intuitive relationship that he and Richardson have always enjoyed, Oliver Stone went with the suggestion. 'Bob challenges Oliver a lot,' said Brian Burden, who had been one of the editors with Hank Corwin on four Oliver Stone films, including *Natural Born Killers*.

> Bob loves to experiment and to try new techniques. And some things work and some don't. But they are very strong-willed people and sometimes there are problems on movies. They do fight. But there's always a lot of respect.

The fact is that Oliver's crew is loyal to him. No other film-maker has this loyal a crew that's been around this long. And it's such a chance to get great material. The shots are just great. I've edited other films with other directors where you're going through all the shots looking for a moment where the camera's switching off or its swinging round by accident – looking for some interesting things to help jazz it up. But Oliver just allows it to happen during a take: asks Bob to pan off and pan back. Or stop the camera. He takes risks. But also Bob pushes Oliver to do new things. Bob does commercials a lot, which is where a lot of experimentation happens. Where he takes some of his toys and tricks from. Different stocks, for example.

In its coagulating of the state-of-mind and state-of-art of our time into a homogeneous whole, *Natural Born Killers* is perhaps the most astonishing picture of the Nineties. Although it is largely written into the script, as it had been in *JFK*, the content of the film is expressed through the rhythm of the editing: the images build a kinetic impression, as in, for example, the explosive final jail sequence. This kinetic perception is delivered through the build-up of the images: Oliver Stone had developed the art of creating images that could be read in a very short time and still deliver the story. It is a visual form akin to the laws of jazz – ironically, considering one of the starting points for this style is considered to be based on the form of rock videos. But whereas the tradition in film previously had been to present a two-dimensional vision, with antecedents that were theatrical or painterly and where the content is behind the frame, in Oliver Stone's most recent work the content is built by the rhythm of the cutting.

In *Natural Born Killers*, moreover, the constant switching of stocks by Bob Richardson assisted this emphasis. Several film stocks were used, including 35mm, super-16, and even 8mm. And various video formats were employed, including Hi-8. Both black-and-white and colour were used in all formats.

One of the most visually fascinating sequences in the film occurs early on: the *I Love Mallory* show, shot as a parody of *I Love Lucy*, in which Mallory's warped psyche is shown to have originated in a background of child abuse. Here Bob Richardson caught the correct period flavour by using a video camera from the Fifties. 'The colours were so garish and disgusting,' said Brian Burden. 'When we did the final colour balance we tried to boost the colours until they were the weirdest we could get.' They succeeded admirably.

For the scene at the end where they kill Wayne Gayle, we lost the entire day's film sound, [Burden added]. They just never shipped it. So there was a video camera running and luckily it had a microphone attached. And we managed to get all the sound using that, because they did a few takes. We had to loop a few things as well. In fact, one of the characters – Wayne Gayle's assistant – is a deaf video producer and we brought her in to look at it to figure out what everybody was saying. Because no-one was following the script exactly.

The rear-screen projection sequences in the film earned much praise. Which obscure French movie was the influence for these? In fact, this concept came from an Alice in Chains video for a song called 'Rooster' that had been directed by Mark Pellington and cut by Hank Corwin.

It was to be another year before *Natural Born Killers* was released, thus allowing for lengthy editing time.

During the mixing stage of the film, Arnold Schwarzenegger was next door, mixing *True Lies*. Walking into the kitchen area one day, Schwarzenegger saw Oliver Stone. 'So,' he said, 'you don't look so good: you need to work out.' 'I *am* working out,' Stone snapped back testily.

In fact, Stone does try and look after himself: he takes regular brisk walks, for example. In Seattle, *Natural Born Killers* was test-screened late one night to the great enjoyment of a fairly select grunge crowd. After the screening Stone went out on the town. But the next morning he could be observed at 8a.m., walking at speed through the city streets.

Natural Born Killers was released in the United States in August 1994. It went straight to number one, and although it soon dropped down the box-office charts it made some $50 million at the US box office.

Reviews on the whole were extremely favourable, epitomized by that of Richard Corliss in *Time*:

Natural Born Killers plunders every visual trick of avante-garde and mainstream cinema...and for two delirious hours, pushes them into your face like a Cagney grapefruit. The actors go hyper hyper, the camera is ever on the bias, the garish colours converge and collide, and you're caught in this Excedrin vision of America in heat. The ride is fun, too, daredevil fun of the sort that only Stone seems willing to provide in this timid film era. *Natural Born Killers* is the most excessive, most exasperating, most...let's just say it's the most movie in quite some time...

Jack Kroll, writing in *Time*'s competitor *Newsweek*, was equally enthusiastic.

The film's multifarious formats are as precisely placed as the planes in a cubist Picasso. The movie is in fact a portrait of a new American mind dislocated and stupefied by vicarious violence. Its extravagant surrealism reflects reality... Stone's besetting fault is sentimentalism, here expressed in his idealization of the redemptive love between Mickey and Mallory. But even here, the performances of Woody Harrelson and Juliette Lewis produce an unsettling passion. The horror is the distortion of that passion to violence: you believe it when the slight Lewis, transfigured by nameless rage, beats the living hell out of some poor rednecks. Stone's flabbergasting movie cannot be dismissed; it must and will be fought over.

The extent of such fighting over *Natural Born Killers*, however, was yet to be fully felt. Before long, 13 copycat murders would be ascribed to young thugs allegedly aping the behaviour of Mickey and Mallory Knox; the film initially was banned in Britain. At the instigation of writer John Grisham, a lawsuit was launched against Oliver Stone by relatives of two people, one murdered, one left paralysed, by Sarah Edmondson and her boyfriend Ben Darras, who had engaged in a crime spree after taking large amounts of LSD and watching *Natural Born Killers*.

Unsurprisingly, Oliver Stone has his own perception of this.

Natural Born Killers will be fresh in 20 years. I don't quite see anyone else making films like that. It's a new grammar. But it was perceived as inciting violence. You can't make films for literal people. They are illusions, and if people want to take them literally, that's their problem. But you can't be responsible on any level for people who take the film and believe it and go out and act. What if someone listens to Beethoven's Fifth Symphony and decides he wants to blow up the world? There's no end given to the interpretations of a piece of work by a literal person.

Movies are illusions. I wanted people to understand where we're at as a society: what's going on. There is an explosion of sensationalism, right up to the OJ trial. Advertisers make a lot of money off this so-called news – it's fake news. It's unimportant. The news is now fucked.

Those who criticize this movie wanted me to do it in a more conventional way, where it's a sober look at it. I think that the hysteria of the film – which was deliberately pitched upward – bothered people.

Grisham went after us in the press, but never sued us. The suit was brought by a Louisiana couple that had been involved in the shooting. One of the victims was paralysed. And they said the two killers had seen the movie. They were friends of Grisham, so he sort of incited a lawsuit. Which I think is a catastrophe to the First Amendment. Again, it's taking the artistic enterprise very literally. You are responsible for murder, Mr Stone, because you created characters who people believe and they go out and they murder. Fine, I'll take that responsibility. My conscience will handle that. But what right do you have to put me behind bars? I don't have anything to do with this murder. I read the Bible the other night: I didn't decide because of that to kill my wife. The Bible is pretty violent. Where does it end?

Grisham is saying that ideas are like defective products. Like refrigerators or cars. He's making a lawsuit out of ideas. Which would be every lawyer's paradise, of course. Grisham is a hypocrite. Because *A Time to Kill* is a vigilante picture. In my opinion, if the Samuel Jackson character had been white, he wouldn't have done it. I've never thought much to Grisham: I've never been able to read one of his books.

In purely artistic terms, James Woods has no doubts whatsoever about the colossal achievement of *Natural Born Killers*: 'Oliver Stone is now making films that show a subjective experience, that have no omniscient point of view. *Natural Born Killers* is as revolutionary as the Gutenberg Bible. This guy is doing work that if it were by Orson Welles would be hailed as genius.'

12 Nixon

It would not be long before James Woods was again working with Oliver Stone. In his enthusiastically thoughtful review of *Natural Born Killers* in *Newsweek*, Jack Kroll had drawn an analogy with the recently published diaries of Richard Nixon's cohort H.R. Haldeman. Parts of them, he wrote,

> read like scenes from a Stone movie. In one, President Nixon and Co. are watching an anti-Vietnam demonstration on TV. Police are using tear gas on demonstrators who are carrying candles. Haldeman writes that Nixon had 'helpful ideas like using helicopters to blow out their candles...said it was like watching an old movie, you keep thinking something interesting will happen.'

Perhaps the notion that the court of disgraced President Richard Nixon was such a surreal world triggered the imagination of Oliver Stone. Before this, however, he had several other productions in mind. The film that had gone furthest down the line was the story of Manual Noriega, the Panamanian strongman deposed after the 1989 US invasion of the Central American country. The story would have needed to operate on several levels simultaneously, including those that connected Noriega's links with Colombian cocaine cartels and the Iran-Contra affair. Although he had carried out extensive research, including a three-hour interview with Noriega, Stone finally decided that the story was too complex for him to come to accurate conclusions that could be simply rendered. It was also said that the director was not happy with the character of the man he had initially believed to be akin to a Creole Bonaparte.

'It was sort of high camp,' said Brian Burden. 'I went to a make-up test for Al Pacino: it was hilarious. Skin make-up, a white captain's suit with a stuffed parrot on his shoulder and a big sabre. Really funny.'

As potential costs escalated towards $50 million, Oliver Stone decided to cancel the project, after a dream 'at four o'clock in the morning. I was in hell.'

Instead, he returned to an earlier idea, the film of the Tim Rice and

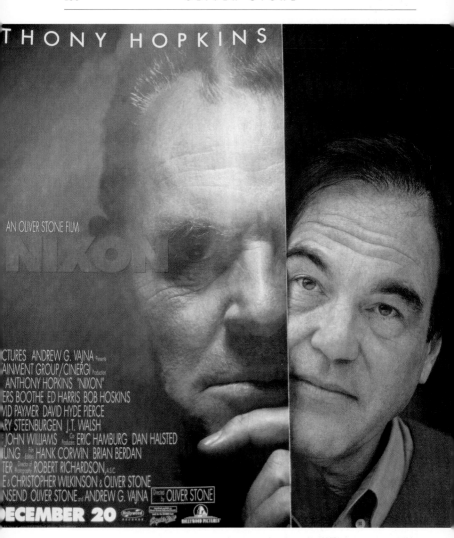

In Nixon, **Stone surprised audiences with a relatively sympathetic portrayal of the disgraced American president, played masterfully by Anthony Hopkins.**

Andrew Lloyd Webber musical *Evita*. Even though he scouted locations in Buenos Aires and had Meryl Streep pencilled in, the film was abandoned.

And there were other ideas in development: a film about forest fire-fighting experiences in the Forties, a spiritual action picture; *The Mayor of Castro Street*, the story of Harvey Milk, the murdered gay mayor of San Francisco; and *Memphis*, the long-discussed film about the assassination of Dr Martin Luther King Jr.

In the end, however, Oliver Stone went with another long-mooted idea: a film about Richard Nixon. This was to have an approach almost like that of a Shakespearian tragedy, portraying the disgraced ex-President as a King Lear-like figure, caught in a psychological miasma he could not escape, until it dragged him to his doom. Nixon's death in April 1994 pushed the idea forward. When Warners passed on the idea, Stone went to Disney with it, and they agreed to put up costs that would eventually total $43 million. Oliver Stone was aware that if he wanted to get another major political film into production, he had better seize the moment – before anyone changed their minds. 'There are few directors this century who have got away with two big political movies that were uncompromised,' he mused.

Born into a working-class, Quaker family in southern California, Richard Nixon transcended his background by becoming a successful lawyer and, after a fiery Red-baiting campaign, winning a seat in Congress. As Republican Vice-President to Eisenhower he might have been expected to walk to victory over the Democrat candidate John F. Kennedy. But he was narrowly defeated – there were always allegations of vote-rigging on the part of the Kennedys – after faring badly in a disastrous televised debate with his far more media-astute opponent. At a subsequent press conference he announced his retirement from politics with the memorable phrase, 'You won't have Richard Nixon to kick around any more,' an expression of an innate paranoia that became a laughing-stock.

In 1968, however, he won the election, becoming President for the Republican party, after campaigning to what became known as the 'Silent Majority', a demographic grouping it seemed he had singlehandedly discovered. While on the one hand appeasing these upholders of traditional values, he also promised to end the involvement in Vietnam, which he singularly failed to do, instead railing against the 'campus bums' who protested over the war, including the four Ohio State students shot to death in 1970 by National Guard troops.

Hampered by an unfortunate personality, Nixon was perceived to be in thrall to Henry Kissinger, his foreign policy adviser and Secretary of State. The President's paranoia seemed to be increasing, an impression that was proven by the pointless Watergate burglary, during the 1972 election. Subsequently it was revealed that many activities within the

White House during Nixon's reign had been captured on tape. Impeached over Watergate, he resigned in disgrace in 1974.

Though the immense insecurities and lack of self-worth that led to his desperate mistakes could suggest otherwise, Richard Nixon was neither arch-villain nor arch-buffoon. In matters of US foreign policy that excluded Vietnam, Nixon's approach was supremely skillful: by giving diplomatic recognition to Mao's China he was not only being realistic, but also creating a balance of power against the Soviet Union that significantly reduced the threat of war. The even-handed George McGovern, Nixon's 'peacenik' Democratic opponent in the 1972 election, generously acknowledged this to Robert Scheer of the *Los Angeles Times*: 'In dealing with the two major Communist powers, Nixon probably had a better record than any President since World War II.' It was Richard Nixon, McGovern told Scheer, who had 'Put us on the course to practical working relationships with both the Russians and Chinese.' Nixon was also the first US President to visit Jerusalem and to treat Arab leaders with respect.

The vision presented in Oliver Stone's film was the director's third differing view of Richard Nixon. As his father's son Stone had supported Nixon in the 1960 election, even wearing a Nixon button. A decade later, after Nixon invaded Cambodia, he considered going to Washington to assassinate him: he would tell his father that the President was a 'very evil man'. Now his view was more balanced.

> Nixon emblemizes much of the American century [Stone told *Premiere* magazine in 1995]. He grew up during the Depression, he went to World War II, and then he participated actively in the Cold War and Vietnam and all the issues of our lifetime. He is what Churchill, in a sense, was for England. And he's a fascinating contradiction – part idealist, part liar.

In fact, there were some parallels between Richard Nixon and Oliver Stone. Both seemed to have been emotionally wounded as children.

To great effect, perhaps because it is so heartfelt, Stone illustrates through the film how his repressed childhood had affected the adult Richard Nixon: there are several sequences documenting the seemingly endless tragedies suffered by the Nixon family and the young Richard Nixon's response to them.

> Nixon never forgave, as opposed to Le Ly Hayslip. That's why Buddhism works, because it allows you to incorporate the hurt, and she learned to forgive her enemies: that's the beauty of *Heaven and Earth*. Whereas Richard Nixon never did. He maintained the Western approach to grudges and revenge: 'Get them for what they did to me.' By the time he entered the White House he was

corrupted already. He was a corrupt person. Corrupted by his bitterness.

Oliver Stone wrote the Nixon script with Stephen J. Rivele and Christoper Wilkinson. Among its moments of controversy were the constant suggestions that Nixon had had a hand in destabilizing and attempting to assassinate Castro. Also, that he was indirectly responsible for the murder of John F. Kennedy. Yet the subtle characterization of the former President came from finer observations: like the moment, taken from Woodward and Bernstein's *The Final Days*, when Nixon becomes so frustrated at not being able to remove the safety cap from a tub of tablets that he bites it off.

The first choice for the part of Richard Nixon had been Warren Beatty. But at a reading of the script at Beatty's house with Oliver Stone and Joan Allen, who was sitting in for Pat Nixon's lines, it became apparent that the director and the potential male lead differed to a substantial degree over the interpretation of Nixon's character. By the end of the evening, it was mutually agreed to proceed no further. As Stone was leaving Beatty's house, however, the actor had a word in his ear. 'Well, it's obvious who should play Nixon's wife, isn't it?' he said, glancing back into the house where Joan Allen still sat.

If the role of Le Ly Hayslip failed to change the views of those who still insisted that Oliver Stone was unable to write parts for women, then surely the Pat Nixon character finally laid the ghost of this hoary old myth. In fact, a central aspect of the complex script hinged around the very human relationship between the President and his wife, endlessly compromising her own existence for the sake of her husband's ambition. (Was Stone drawing here on his own relationship with Elizabeth?) 'Nixon is as much a love story as anything,' said Stone.

Finally Oliver Stone settled on the great Welsh actor Anthony Hopkins to play Richard Nixon. Going on the director's media reputation, Anthony Hopkins had expected 'a kind of caveman'. As is so often the case, he found instead someone who was the opposite of his reputation: like so many people who have reputations for being 'difficult', Oliver Stone simply knows what he wants.

So convincing was Hopkins that almost as soon as he came on screen you believed that this was the desperately flawed Richard Nixon. Having thoroughly immersed himself in researching his character, he presented a figure of deep, empathetic pathos.

I've tried to find compassion and a sympathy for his loneliness, his isolation. I think that he felt like an outsider all his life [Hopkins told *Premiere*]. ...I wouldn't say we've trashed Nixon at all. I am protective. He was a human being. I

Anthony Hopkins had expected Oliver Stone to be a 'kind of caveman'; he was pleasantly surprised.

wouldn't say that of Hitler or Stalin, but Nixon – whatever he did – he was a human being. I mean, he was an astonishing man. To think what he did! He opened up the Communist world. His vision for domestic policy and civil rights, the environment and welfare and health reform were very good. They've been overshadowed by Watergate.

Again, Oliver Stone had come up with a masterful performance for a lead role.

People would come up to me and say, 'I can't believe it: you made me like that bastard,' [he said to me]. It's a very tricky film, and again it defies a stereotype. Those people who did see it from the left or from the centre were amazed at how empathetic he was. Probably overly empathetic to Nixon. Because it was the nature of drama to do that. Anthony Hopkins had that capacity to generate warmth, which the real Richard Nixon had a hard time doing.

As he had with *JFK*, Stone came up with a panoply of star performers to pull audiences into this epic film. As well as Joan Allen playing Pat Nixon, Bob Hoskins was cast as J. Edgar Hoover, Ed Harris as Howard Hunt, Paul Sorvino as Henry Kissinger, Powers Boothe as White House Chief-of-Staff General Alexander Haig, and James Woods as H. R. Haldeman.

Initially, Stone had wanted Powers Boothe to play Haldeman. James Woods, however, showed him what he could bring to the part, one of steely, crewcut, semi-psychotic nerviness. Woods noted how actors' rehearsals with Oliver Stone had moved on since he'd played the part of Richard Boyle in *Salvador*. Now Stone seemed to be working more in the freeform manner of, say, Mike Leigh.

We sat around for three to four weeks coming up with stuff, like the confrontational scenes [said Woods]. The king and his court. Paul Sorvino and I found a way to make the animosity work and stay friends. Through this process the scenes got to be greatly rewritten.

Oliver works and rehearses with the actors at length. And Bob Richardson comes in and works out how to get what emerges on camera. I don't know any other director who does this.

We'd always rehearse in costume. Bob would walk around with a hand-held black-and-white camera, like D.A. Pennebaker, shooting everything. And in the film you're constantly being jarred out of your complacency by this documentary-like footage.

Richardson wove further magic in the film with a hand-crank camera he had.

We used it in a lot of the flashback stuff in *Nixon* [said Brian Burden], the child-hood stuff, where it stutters and it goes to the image. What he's doing is he's hand-cranking and the camera's shaking, and he'll back the film up and he'll go forward again. So you'll get a ghost of the image, like an in-camera dissolve. It would be far too expensive to do that optically. Although you could do it in post. But it's much cooler if you can find the bits to do it in camera.

There were a few scenes where we wanted some heightened tension by panning back and forth off a character on certain words. And half or even three-quarters of the time it didn't work at all. It was almost unusable. But there were a few moments when the synch of the movement and the synch of the performance hit and they were magic.

Nixon was shot almost entirely on a sound stage in Los Angeles, with a minimum of location filming in Long Beach and Washington DC for establishing footage.

Shortly before *Nixon* was released at the end of 1995, Stone's girlfriend Chong Son Chong, a Korean actress and model, gave birth to Tara (named for the Buddhist deity of compassion), a daughter for Oliver Stone.

This was to prove greater cause for celebration than the success of the film, however: *Nixon* only took in $26 million at the US box office; although overseas sales put it into the black, it was certainly not a hit.

Oliver Stone, moreover, was once again embroiled in controversy. He was attacked by the late President's daughters, Tricia Nixon Cox and Julie Nixon Eisenhower, who decried the film as 'character assassination'. ('They never saw the film at the time,' said Stone. 'So they are not opening their minds.') In a letter to these two women, Diane Disney Miller wrote that she was ashamed of her father's company being associated with the film; she labelled it 'a grave disservice to your family, to the presidency and to American history'.

And there was more. 'This is a vicious attack,' said Alexander Haig. 'It is a despicable fairy tale,' said former Treasury Secretary William Simon.

Perhaps understandably, George McGovern had a different point of view. He drew attention, for example, to where Oliver Stone says in the film that Vietnam was a domestic US issue – McGovern said that he had had it confirmed to him by Kissinger that Nixon couldn't end the Vietnam war, because the right wing would have rebelled. The former Presidential candidate drew attention to the scene in which a 19-year-old girl says to Nixon, 'You can't end the war – the system won't let you.' And he described how Nixon then went back to the White House and told his wife that the girl was right. This, McGovern insisted, was the truth.

I don't think Nixon meant it when he said in 1968 that he was going to end the war [said Stone]. I think it was a cynical plan. I think he might have put out the word to undermine the Peace Talks in Paris while Johnson was still in office. I think that he and Kissinger were very practical about it: the terms that were offered in 1969 were essentially the same terms accepted in '73. So I think he extended the war purely for political reasons. As Johnson did. But Nixon and Kissinger knew that they could not win. There was no question about that. It was, how can you get out without losing? Without the right wing making a patsy out of you? And that seems to have been what concerned Nixon: that he would alienate the right and the military.

I've made mistakes in details. I really believed in what I said in *JFK* and *Nixon*. But I think I made many mistakes in details. People have nailed me for it. Or tried to. But I don't think that defeated the overall truth about what was being said. I don't think the details were that major, by the way. But there were some slip-ups. But I do my homework. I did a lot of reading, a lot of research on those movies. I am responsible to myself. I have my own ethic. I read as much as I can across the spectrum of the subject of what I write about.

Real life is complicated. Much more so than any film could ever be. As I said at the time, Nixon's decisions were based on 73 phone calls in 42 different places. It was much more complex. But in a movie you reduce it to one decision at one time with five faces or whatever: you have to. Decisions are made over a period of time. Most actions take place over a period of time. Very rarely in a dramatic moment. In a close-up.

Once you have an interpretation, once you allow an actor to do the movie, once you art direct the design, once you have a script, you're into a realm of interpretation – the actor interprets the real person. So the distinction that's been made is wrong. Every movie has an interpretation. Historians throw facts at me all the time. Facts are very precious things. Facts are sometimes erroneous. Sometimes the facts have been badly reported. It would be great to know everything.

James Woods, meanwhile, has his own memorable perception of the constant attacks meted out to Oliver Stone:

The question I ask is, would the world of cinema or politics be a better or worse place with or without Oliver Stone? The answer is obvious.

You have the cinema of the westerns of John Ford or the gangster films of Francis Ford Coppola which are great films, but where the level of fantasy is almost laughable. Yet I've been with Oliver when he's been researching films and I've seen the level of detail that he goes into. On *Nixon*, for example, where I was with him for about three or four weeks of the research. And of course you'll have composite characters and condensed scenes. But the essential truth is there in a dramatic form.

Yet we have a situation where, when *Nixon* came out, Henry Kissinger wrote an article in the *New York Times* in which his criticisms of the film were based essentially on the fact that he had never smoked cigars as he was portrayed doing in the film.

Oliver takes a provocative, skewed approach to comfortable history – he attacks this cast-iron view of history – and they are so afraid that the Golden Cow will come tumbling down. It's nothing new: people were pissed off when Einstein announced that Newtonian physics was essentially flawed and incorrect. And because Oliver has this sybaritic lifestyle he's easy to attack by the liberal press.

But I'd rather that Oliver was making *JFK* than *Batman 6*. How many film-makers would make a $40 million film about Richard Nixon? But the attitude adopted by so many people towards Oliver Stone simply proves the old adage that no good deed goes unpunished. The sheep don't like it when the wolf is having too much fun.

Yet no one credits him with redefining the grammar of film. Look at the progress he's made up to *Nixon*. There are some great film-makers out there, but he is the most unique film-maker there is. In the future Oliver Stone, Orson Welles, and Sergei Eisenstein will be seen as having been the three key players in defining the parameters of the grammar of film, both as a history lesson and as pure entertainment.

13 Stray Dogs

For Christmas release in the United States in 1996 Oliver Stone produced *The People vs Larry Flynt*: the story of the controversial porn tycoon who was shot and paralysed not long after offering a million dollars to anyone who would bring proof of who killed John F. Kennedy.

Directed by Milos Forman and starring Woody Harrelson and Courtney Love, the film soon attracted a barrage of attacks from people claiming it glorified the degradation of women. What Stone had actually picked up on, however, was that Flynt was a fascinating subject, another alternative American figurehead.

> I produce a movie with Milos Forman. We bring him back, he's been seven or eight years away. He was very happy: he had this movie given to him. And all I get from it is, 'Thank God Oliver Stone didn't direct this movie. It would have been way over the top.' They don't even give me credit as co-producer of the movie. It was actually Scott and Larry's idea [the writers], it wasn't mine. They came to me and said, 'You're perfect for Larry Flynt.' I didn't get it right away. But once they wrote it I understood it: certainly he fits into the scumbag gallery I've come up with. I think Larry Flynt is a much misunderstood man – like I am.

Perhaps as an antidote to much of his previous subject-matter, Oliver Stone's next choice of subject-matter was *Stray Dogs*, originally called *U-turn*, a noir-comedy ('film soleil', as Stone termed it) with shades of spaghetti western as well as shaggy dog story. Shot on Seventies military test film, it has a look that matches its mood. Written by John Ridley, it had had its script re-worked by Stone and Richard Rutowski.

Starring Sean Penn, Nick Nolte, and Jennifer Lopez, playing husband and wife, it was still a work-in-progress in the spring of 1997.

> *U-turn* is another kind of movie [said Stone]. It pays homage to the conventions of the film noir of the Forties. But I'm trying to deal with it in the Nineties. It's a series of looks, feelings, about betrayal, jealousy, and trust, and people who make choices. Set in a small town in the South-west. There are only about

Woody Harrelson and Courtney Love in The People vs Larry Flynt**, the Oliver Stone produced story of another American anti-hero.**

six or seven people in there, and they all get interrelated during the course of the movie. Because a drifter comes to town and his radiator hose breaks. And everybody gets into this interlocked dance. And everybody acts out their thing. And it evolves into murder – money, sex, betrayal. There's a dark side to me, always has been.

U-turn might be a surprise to some people. Because it's more of a genre piece. It's easy; it's not torturing you. It's good for me to make a film that has fun. At the same time there is some depth to it.

The pill-popping drifter, Bobby Cooper, played by Sean Penn, is having a series of Bad Days and finds himself hired by both Nolte, playing Jake McKenna like a cross between Lee Marvin and Humphrey Bogart in *The Treasure of the Sierra Madre* (Stone has mooted doing a re-make of this classic), and Lopez – each wanting him to kill the other.

The unconventional cutting at the beginning of the film was reminiscent in its illogical juxtaposition of shot angles of the economical editing of Godard's *À Bout de Souffle*. With a final act filled with corkscrew-like twists that had you on the edge of your seat, you were still aware that there was plenty of room for tightening the narrative drive in the long middle sequence; this was despite a gripping murder scene (*A Shorter Film About Killing*) and the thrilling subsequent escape from the Arizona town of Superior in which the picture is set.

I love editing, [said Oliver Stone]. What we're doing now in *U-turn* is exactly like this. The script was working and read well on paper. We acted it out and it worked there. How come it doesn't work on film? [Laughs.] So I'm rewriting. I'm removing a lot of dialogue. I'm saying I never thought the scene would be able to work without that line of dialogue. But it does. You don't have to say some things that just get said somehow. So what is it that gets said? There's always that question that makes films for me so eternally vivid or fresh. It's that each time you come back to these essential questions of: do you really need to say that? And everything is up for grabs – 'Hello.' 'Goodbye.' 'Thank you.' 'I'm sorry.' 'Fuck me.' 'I love you.' Every fucking line is subject to interpretation. Is it valid? Is it real? In most conditions if you live that way you add it yourself. In real life too. What am I saying to you now? Why am I doing this interview? Why am I eating dinner? What is my life about? Why have I put one foot in front of the next one? What is it all about, Alfie?

I've always thought the three parts – writing, directing, and editing – are wonderful. They are all activities of a different nature, but they complement each other. Writing is unto itself – it's solitary. I love being solitary. I love the quiet. I love living inside. Directing is wholly, full-out, creative on all fronts. A director is also an actor, he's a writer, he's a general, he should be an editor in his head. He should see it all coming. A director will never be satisfied because he can never do it right. In life it's inevitable that a thousand different solutions are available, and he always feels like he's only used three or something. So the director always has the fatal flaw of being the tragic figure, never consummating, if that's the right word. And editing is another form completely unto itself. It's also a form of writing, because you can take the writing and restructure it very cleverly in ways that you never imagined when you were writing it. I always find I think, 'Why didn't I think of that when I was writing it?' It really bugs me. So it pays off the writing: the writing is a seed, and the editing pays off planting the seed.

Each time I make a movie I become somebody else. I become the style of the movie in a sense. My wife used to say at that time that I change my clothes with each movie: in the Morrison phase I was much younger in my head; in the Nixon phase I was an older man – I got fatter. Each time I was like my own Method director cut. I'd become the subject. And it's interesting in the reviews you read: each time they will make me into Jim Morrison and they'll tear me down as Jim Morrison or Richard Nixon or Jim Garrison on a crusade or as Ronnie Kovic – saying that I have no sense of humour and so on. So I wonder how can I be all these people at the end of the day. Who am I? They are missing the point. They don't know who Oliver Stone is: they have no fucking idea. Oliver Stone is still a mystery – to me too.

THE

REVIEWS

THE HAND

Wednesday, April 29, 1981

For Fright Freaks
Hollywood, April 21.
Orion Pictures release through Warner Bros. of an Edward R. Pressman-Ixtlan production. Produced by Edward R. Pressman. Directed by Oliver Stone. Features entire cast. Exec producer, Clark L. Paylow. Screenplay, Stone, based on the book "The Lizard's Tail;" camera (Technicolor), King Baggot; editor, Richard Marks; music, James Horner; production design, John Michael Riva; special visual effects, Carlo Rambaldi; sound, Darin Knight; assistant director, Kim Kurumada. Reviewed at The Burbank Studios, L.A., April 21, 1981. (MPAA Rating: R.) Running time: 104 mins. (Color)

Jon Lansdale	Michael Caine
Anne Lansdale	Andrea Marcovicci
Stella Roche	Annie McEnroe
Brian Ferguson	Bruce McGill
Doctress	Viveca Lindfors
Karen Wagner	Rosemary Maurphy
Lizzie Lansdale	Mara Hobel
Sheriff	Pat Corley
Bill Richman	Nicholas Hormann

There is something inherently amusing about a severed hand with enough gumption to murder any number of silly, unsympathetic people cast opposite it in a major motion picture. But that's one of the only plusses of "The Hand," Orion's latest entry into the thriller sweepstakes. Not only is this Edward R. Pressman production seldom scary, it lacks any of the real ingenuity (or blood) needed to hook filmgoers who have been frightened by almost every creature and thing imaginable. Genre fans should provide some initial business but any hope beyond that

is, pardon the pun, reaching.

Director-scripter Oliver Stone takes on a premise – that of an autonomous appendage wreaking havoc on anyone crossing the human it was¹ previously attached to – that has in some form been effectively executed in many past pix. However, he focuses much too closely and literally on the hand itself for it to seem like a seriously imposing villain.

In reality, it is perversely funny to view this small hand scurrying around the floor or skulking in corners awaiting its next victim. And the visual image of it bringing a fully grown man to his knees is akin to sitting center ring for a wrestling match between Tweetie Pie and Dumbo.

There is little relief to be found from the relationships in the script. Cartoonist Michael Caine and his soul-searching wife, Andrea Marcovicci, don't get along almost from the start, and they become a tiresome pair as the film progresses. Although Caine evokes some sympathy after he loses his hand and particularly in scenes with daughter Mara Hobel, he spends most of his time sweating and grimacing into the camera lens. It's not a pretty sight.

Annie McEnroe, Bruce McGill, Viveca Lindfors and Pat Corley limn [draw] various offbeat characters who are either lackadaisacal or laughable, probably without intending to be. They make one want to root for the hand.

Special visual effects consultant Carlo Rambaldi, who performed wonders on "Alien," should probably share some of the blame for the ineffectiveness of the aforementioned villain. Most other tech credits are okay but nothing really special.

Exception is James Horner, who has concocted an appropriately haunting score throughout. But ironically his work serves to point up just how devoid of any sustained suspense "The Hand" really is.

Berg

SALVADOR

Wednesday, March 5 1986

Controversial, semi-docu drama of a photojournalist in Central America.

A Hemdale release and presentation. Produced by Gerald Green, Oliver Stone. Executive producers, John Daly, Derek Gibson. Directed by Stone. Stars James Woods. Screenplay, Stone, Richard Boyle, camera (color), Robert Richardson; editor, Claire Simpson; music, Georges Delerue; production design, Bruno Rubeo; art direction, (Mexico), Melo Hinojosa; costume design, Kathryn Greko Morrison; special effects supervision, Yves De Bono; associate producers, Bob Morones, Brad H. Aronson; assistant directors, Ramon Menendez, Jose Luis Ortega (Mexico). Reviewed at the Avco Cinema, W. Los Angeles, Feb. 23, 1986. (MPAA Rating: R.) Running time: 123 mins. (Color)

Richard Boyle	James Woods
Dr. Rock	James Belushi
Amb. Thomas Kelly	Michael Murphy
John Cassady	John Savage
Maria	Elpedia Carrillo
Major Max	Tony Plana
Jack Morgan	Colby Chester
Cathy Moore	Cynthia Gibb
Col. Hyde	Will MacMillian
Pauline Axelrod	Valerie Wildman
Archbishop Romero	Jose Carlos Ruiz
Col. Julio Figueroa	Jorge Luke
Army Lieutenant	Juan Fernandez

Hollywood – The tale of American photojournalist Richard Boyle's adventures in strife-torn Central America five years ago, "Salvador" is as raw, difficult, compelling, unreasonable, reckless and vivid as its protagonist. Oliver Stone's picture, which had its world premiere at the Santa Barbara Intl. Film Festival on Feb. 28, will serve as the first release of Hemdale's distribution arm, and the b.o. [box office] road will not be easy. Contemporary political pictures in general, and those on Central America in particular, such as "Under Fire" and "Latino," have not appealed to the public. There's plenty here to provoke discussion, enough to spark sufficient controversy to give the film a foot in the door of the specialized and art market.

Designed to expose as many outrages, injustices and human tragedies as possible, pic naturally comes down savagely upon the Salvadoran military, the Death Squads, and U.S. government backing or tolerance for at least some of their excesses. Nevertheless, it would be far from accurate to label this a left-wing tract.

Despite a brief sequence which embarrassingly idealizes the peasant insurgents, Stone seems anxious to straddle the political fence. He makes sure to point out that the left can be just as brutal as the right, and seems to conclude by saying that Central America is such a chaotic mess that no coherent attitude or policy is possible until a return to some basic human values is effected. Indeed, nothing in Stone's previous filmography ("Midnight Express," "Scarface," "Year Of The Dragon") would lead one to believe that he stands in the forefront of Hollywood's liberal-left humanists.

James Woods portrays the real-life Boyle, who at the outset is shown to be at his lowest ebb as a virtual bum and professional outcast in San Francisco.

With no particular prospects, he shanghais fun-loving buddy James Belushi for the long drive down to (El) Salvador, where Woods has left behind a native girlfriend and where he thinks he might be able to pick up some freelance work.

Hard to warm up to because of his extreme irresponsibility, crudeness and irrepressible need to take advantage of everyone in sight for selfish reasons, Woods/Boyle nevertheless cuts an amusing figure as he bumps up against glowering Death Squad officers, double-talking U.S. Embassy types, self-righteous military officers and priggish, clean-cut establishment reporters.

A man of such manic energy and mighty enthusiasm that even vast quantities of alcohol can't douse the flames, Woods finally sobers up when he discovers the true magnitude of suffering going on in the country he formerly visited for its great surfing and pretty women.

The film's major problem as a story is that its course feels determined by historical events, rather than by the imperatives of good dramatic structure. Stone makes sure his hero is present at every conceivable moment of significance – a 1980 U.S. Embassy party where Ronald Reagan's election is celebrated, the assassination of Archbishop Romero, the immediate aftermath of the rape and murder of the American nuns, a decisive battle between the government and rebels – but hasn't adequately shaped matters to artistic ends.

Woods' transition comes too abruptly, Belushi virtually disappears from the story, and Stone unfortunately allows his spokesman to figuratively mount a platform and, for many sanctimonious minutes, tell off American government personnel and chastise them for their lack of "human decency," when he himself is a walking illustration of incivility.

Nevertheless, the film has an immediacy, energy and vividness that is often quite exciting, and the essential truth of much of what Stone has put on display will prove bracing for many viewers. Except for his occasional missteps, the director rivets the attention in scene after scene.

Working in a documentary-like style, Stone, lenser [cameraman] Robert Richardson and production designer

Bruno Rubeo have very effectively caught the teeming confusion, appalling poverty, natural beauty and festering danger of this Third World region.

Woods and Boyle seem to go together like hand and glove. It's unimaginable that any actor could be more convincing as such a crazed, impassioned correspondent. John Savage pops in from time to time as a combat photographer who wants to be Robert Capa and finally gets his wish. Michael Murphy feels right as the outgoing U.S. ambassador, and remainder of the cast is uniformly good.

Despite the dramatic problems, Stone has gotten a great deal of visual and political material up on the screen, and it's all worth grappling with. A fine point: Woods' repeated use of the term "yuppies," a category of people he naturally can't stand, is decidedly premature in 1980.

Cart

PLATOON

Wednesday, December 3, 1986.

Flawed study of men in war.

An Orion Pictures release of a Hemdale Film Corp. presentation of an Arnold Kopelson production. Produced by Kopelson. Coproducer, A. Kitman Ho. Executive producers, John Daly, Derek Gibson. Production executive, Pierre David. Written and directed by Oliver Stone. Stars Tom Berenger, Willem Dafoe, Charlie Sheen. Camera (CFI color), Robert Richardson; editor, Claire Simpson; music, Georges Delerue; production design, Bruno Rubeo; art direction, Rodel Cruz, Doris Sherman Williams; special effects supervisor, Yves de Bono; special makeup effects, visual continuity, Gordon J. Smith; sound (Dolby), Simon Kaye; assistant director, H. Gordon Boos; second unit camera, Tom Sigel; casting, Pat Golden, Bob Morones, Warren McLean. Reviewed at the Samuel Goldwyn Theater, Beverly Hills, Nov. 18, 1986. (MPAA Rating: R.) Running time: 120 mins. (Color)

Sergeant Barnes	Tom Berenger
Sergeant Elias	Willem Dafoe
Chris	Charlie Sheen
Big Harold	Forest Whitaker
Rhah	Francesco Quinn
Sergeant O'Neill	John C. McGinley
Sal	Richard Edson
Bunny	Kevin Dillon
Junior	Reggie Johnson
King	Keith David
Lerner	Johnny Depp
Tex	David Neidorf

Hollywood – "Platoon" is an intense but artistically distanced study of infantry life during the Vietnam War. Writer-director Oliver Stone seeks to immerse the audience totally in the nightmare of the United States' misguided adventure, and manages to do so in a number of very effective scenes. But his set of dual impulses – to stun the viewer with a brutal immediacy on the one hand, and to assert a reflective sense of artistic hindsight on the other – dilutes whatever the film was meant to say, and takes the edge off its power. Commercial prospects look okay, better than that if it reaps some strong critical notices.

A Vietnam vet himself, Stone obviously had urgent personal reasons for making this picture, a fact that emerges instantly as green volunteer Charlie Sheen is plunged into the thick of action along the Cambodian border in late 1967.

Unit with which he's placed is broken down into three rough categories of men: the macho, might-is-right tough guys led by heavily scarred Sergeant Tom Berenger, the marginally more intelligent pot-heads whose ostensible figurehead is doubting war veteran Willem Dafoe, and assorted loners who just hope to get by by watching out for their own skins.

Sheen soon is adopted by the dopers, and the long periods of waiting for action are fraught with dissension among the groups, a conflict epitomized by the rivalry between Berenger, the unreflective man of action, and Dafoe, a man of conscience who learns from experience.

Most traumatic sequence, which will shock many viewers through its exposé of shameful and unprovoked American brutality, has the unit taking a tiny village where local farmers are suspected of hiding and aiding the Vietcong. The G.I.s mercilessly murder a young man, terrorize the entire populace, and gang rape a young girl, among other atrocities, treatment that provokes a complete split between the group's two main factions and paves the way for further senselessness and tragedy.

Also striking is a long scene of the men at play, drinking, getting high and dancing, that nicely points up the unnatural aspects of this enforced all-male society, as well as the climactic, nocturnal battle which becomes a hideous slaughter.

Where Stone's previous effort, "Salvador," was hot and explosive, however, despite its flaws, "Platoon" is cool and never goes quite as far as one imagines it will. All the images in the earlier film seemed caught on the run under extreme pressure, while all the beautiful and undoubtedly difficult moving camera shots here express a sense of grace and precision that removes the visceral quality from the violence.

One is forcibly reminded of "Apocalypse Now" throughout because of the presence centerscreen of Charlie Sheen, who bears a remarkable resemblance here to his father, star of Francis Coppola's epic.

Otherwise, however, "Platoon" in form resembles the taut, close-up army unit films of the 1950s such as Anthony Mann's "Men In War," Robert Aldrich's "Attack!" and Samuel Fuller's "The Steel Helmet" and "Fixed Bayonets". Despite its violence and barrage of realistically dirty language, "Platoon" could have used some of these films' ferociousness, starkness and unpretentiousness. The artistic veneer Stone applies, along with the simpy narration provided for Sheen in the way of letters to his grandmother, detract significantly from the work's immediacy.

Nevertheless, there is plenty of good work to be found here, and pic certainly grabs the viewer by the collar in a way not found everyday in contemporary films. Working on an undoubtedly modest budget in the Philippines (lensing [filming] started just as President Aquino was replacing Marcos), team has mounted an impressive-looking production in all respects, although cinematographer Robert Richardson overdoes the filters at times. Georges Delerue's plaintive score consists largely of a new arrangement of Samuel Barber's "Adagio For Strings."

Willem Dafoe comes close to stealing the picture as the sympathetic sergeant whose drugged state may even heighten his sensitivity to the insanity around him, and each of the members of the young cast have their moments to shine.

Stone implicitly suggests the U.S. lost the war because of divisions within its own ranks and an unwillingness to go all the way, which leaves one with the tragic result that all the suffering and trauma was for nothing. Unfortunately, the analysis here goes no further than that; better if Stone had stuck to combat basic.

Cart

WALL STREET

Wednesday, December 9, 1987

Oliver Stone stumbles with a lecture instead of entertainment.

A 20th Century Fox release of an Edward R. Pressman production, in association with American Entertainment Partners L.P. Produced by Pressman. Co-produced by A. Kitman Ho. Directed by Oliver Stone. Stars Michael Douglas, Charlie Sheen. Screenplay, Stone, Stanley Weiser; camera (DeLuxe color), Robert Richardson; editor, Claire Simpson; music, Stewart Copeland; production design, Stephen Hendrickson; art direction, John Jay Moore, Hilda Stark; set decoration, Leslie Bloom, Susan Bode; costume design, Ellen Mirojnick; sound (Dolby), Chris Newman; associate producer, Michael Flynn; assistant director, Steve Lim; casting, Risa Bramon, Billy Hopkins. Reviewed at 20th Century Fox screening room, Culver City, Calif. Dec. 3, 1987. (MPAA Rating: R). Running time: 124 mins. (Color)

Bud Fox	Charlie Sheen
Gordon Gekko	Michael Douglas
Carl Fox	Martin Sheen
Sir Larry Wildman	Terence Stamp
Kate Gekko	Sean Young
Darien Taylor	Daryl Hannah
Realtor	Sylvia Miles
Roger Barnes	James Spader

Also with: Hal Holbrook, John McGinley, Saul Rubinek, Frankin Cover, James Karen, Richard Dysart, Josh Mostel, Millie Perkins, Annie McEnroe, Monique van Vooren.

Hollywood — Watching Oliver Stone's "Wall Street" is about as wordy and dreary as reading the financial papers accounts of the rise and fall of an Ivan Boesky-type arbitrageur, with one exception. Instead of editorializing about the evils of greed — and greenmailers in particular — it lectures, which is great as a case study in business school but wearisome as a film. Even with the attachment of Stone's "Platoon" reputation and a big name cast, this is a bull holiday market for new issues and "Wall Street" appears an unlikely blue chip entry.

The lure of making a bundle on Wall Street by the young broker (Charlie Sheen) totally seduced by the power and financial stature of such a megalomaniacal arbitrageur as Gordon Gekko (Michael Douglas) is as good a contemporary story as there is today in the real world of takeovers and mergers.

Core problem with this filmed version is that it is too thorough a retelling of the impact, more like a docu-drama than a drama.

Pic needs to be edited by a good 30 minutes (it runs just over two hours) to cut the extraneous, repetitive scenes with Douglas barking orders to buy, sell and run his competitors into the ground or otherwise delivering one of his declamatory speeches on how greed is what makes America great.

Stone and co-writer Stanley Weiser seem to be have done their research on the details of how greenmailers achieve their dubious aims with a script that goes over the process step by step in wordy expositions — diluting the human consequences such actions have on the targeted airline company and its employees (led by Martin Sheen).

Film instead focuses on the cold, calculating and clichéd Douglas character and his eager protégé Sheen Jr. and their love-hate relationship on the treadmill of avarice with settings on the trading floor, in chi-chi restaurants and out in the fashionable Hamptons ringing pretty much true.

Douglas is a nasty enough manipulator and exudes the black-hearted temperament suited to his role, though his character could have used a little shading. Trouble is, Sheen comes off as a pawn in Douglas' corporate raider game and as the easily duped sort doesn't elicit much sympathy since he is only remorseful once Douglas cheats on him and changes the rules of play. Martin Sheen as his father, the airplane mechanic, is the only person worth caring about. Dramatizing the triangle among him, his son and Douglas would have been a more effective presentation of the consequences of greenmailing than cold, dispassionate scenes where it's talked about in a way that results in little emotional impact.

This is also true of Sheen Jr.'s relationship to an ambitious interior decorator, Daryl Hannah, who has no conscience to speak of and the personality of wallboard. She gets short shrift when it comes to intelligence and charm, as do the other two main female characters – Douglas' ditzy wife (Sean Young) and the loud New Yawk realtor (Sylvia Miles) – in "Wall Street's" male dominated world.

The moralizing is done by secondary characters like Hal Holbrook, sage of the trading floor, and at least one of Sheen's fellow brokers, John McGinley, who rightly calls his colleague an "a.h." to his face.

Best elements of Stone's latest work are in the production values, reuniting several parties from "Platoon."

Dizzying pace of Manhattan comes through in Robert Richardson's constantly moving camera, adding to the documentary look of the picture. Production designer Stephen Hendrickson has a keen eye for authenticity – whether it be Douglas' vast corporate offices chock-a-block with expensive modern art or in the crammed working quarters that is the trading floor of the fictitious Jackson-Steinem investment house where Sheen and rows of others go cross-eyed reading the financial tables on their VDTs and hoarse screaming orders into the phone.

Brit

TALK RADIO

December 7–13, 1988

A Universal Pictures release of a Cineplex Odeon Films presentation of an Edward R. Pressman production in association with Ten Four Prods. Executive producers, Greg Strangis, Sam Strangis. Produced by Pressman, A. Kitman Ho. Directed by Oliver Stone. Screenplay, Eric Bogosian, Stone, based on the play "Talk Radio" created by Bogosian, Tad Savinar, written by Bogosian, and the book "Talked To Death: The Life And Murder Of Alan Berg" by Stephen Singular; camera (Deluxe color; the Film House Group prints), Robert Richardson; editor, David Brenner; coeditor, Joe Hutshing; music, Stewart Copeland; sound (Dolby), Tod A. Maitland; production design, Bruno Rubeo; art direction, Milo; set decoration, Derek R. Hill; costume design, Ellen Mirojnick; associate producers, Diane Schneier, Neal Weisman; assistant director, Joseph Reidy; casting, Risa Bramon, Billy Hopkins. Reviewed at Carolco Screening Room, L.A., Nov. 21, 1988. MPAA Rating: R. Running time: 110 mins.

Barry Champlain	Eric Bogosian
Dan	Alec Baldwin
Ellen	Ellen Greene
Laura	Leslie Hope
Stu	John C. McGinley
Chuck Dietz	John Pankow
Kent	Michael Wincott
Sid Greenberg	Zach Grenier
Woman at basketball game	
	Anna Levine
Jeffrey Fisher	Robert Trebor
Sheila Fleming	Linda Atkinson
Vince	Allan Corduner

"Talk Radio" casts a spotlight on the unpalatable underside of American public opinion, and turns up an unlimited supply of anger, hatred and resentment in the process.

Superbly directed by Oliver Stone and pungently performed by Eric Bogosian, author of the original play of the same name, this will primarily appeal to serious, upscale filmgoers interested in Stone and the issues in question, but could break out to a wider audience due to the current fascination for confrontational media programs – the format that provides the context for the picture.

Known in theatrical circles as a monologist and performance artist, Bogosian debuted the initial incarnation of "Talk Radio" in Portland, Ore., in 1985, and last year starred in a well-received expanded version at the Public Theater in New York. For the screenplay, he and Stone worked on material relating to Alan Berg, the Denver talkshow host murdered by neo-Nazis in 1984, and also created a flashback to illuminate their antihero's personal background and beginnings in the radio game.

Most of the film, however, unfolds in the modern studio of KGAB, a Dallas station from which the infamous Barry Champlain holds forth. Young, caustic, rude, insulting, grandstanding, flippant,

Original Play

N.Y. Shakespeare Festival/Joseph Papp presentation of a play in one act by Eric Bogosian, based on an idea by Ted Savinar. Staged by Frederick Zollo. Settings, David Jenkins; visual graphics, Ted Savinar; costumes, Pilar Limosner; lighting, Jan Kroeze; associate producer, Jason Steven Cohen; stage managers, Alan R. Traynor, Pat Sosnow; general managers, Laurel Ann Wilson, Robert MacDonald; publicity, Richard Kornberg, Opened May 28, 1987 at the Public/Martinson Hall, N.Y., $25 top. *Cast:* Linda Atkinson, Eric Bogosian, William DeAcutis, Susan Gabriel, Zach Grenier, Michaele M. Mariana, John C. McGinley, Mark Metcalf, Peter Onorati, Robyn Peterson, Michael Wincott.

and mercilessly cruel, the talkshow host spews vitriol impartially on those of all races, colors and creeds, spares the feelings of no one and specializes in quickly identifying and then picking up on people's vulnerabilities and handicaps.

Partly because he attracts the afflicted, Champlain draws out the nighttime's seamiest denizens from under their rocks, fringe characters whose access to the airwaves gives them a platform for their loony views and who collectively constitute a disturbing portrait of the American mentality.

For their trouble, of course, the callers absorb a torrent of abuse from Champlain, but the public also takes advantage of his appearance at a local basketball game to turn the tables, booing him so vociferously he must beat a hasty retreat.

A dramatic structure has been imposed on the proceedings by the arrival of a radio syndicator who wants to take Champlain's show nationwide. Instead of greeting this news happily, however, the host takes extra bottles of acid off his shelf and showers everyone with it, so distrustful is he of this potential new overload.

At the same time, Champlain's ex-wife Ellen (Ellen Greene) arrives in town, which occasions a look back at the man's origins in the clothing business, his immediate success on the air when invited on as a guest, his change to a non-Jewish name, and the destruction of his marriage due to his infidelity and mean thoughtlessness.

Ellen's presence also allows for the most probing exploration into the astonishing depth of Champlain's anger and self-loathing, but this attempt at creating a psychological portrait of the man falls rather short of truly explaining the roots of his aggressive behavior.

Along the way, the most prominent recurring motif relates to racism and, more specifically, anti-Semitism. Redneck callers complain about Jews and persistently threaten Champlain over his religion. It is against his instincts to take these crackpots seriously, but any viewer familiar with the Alan Berg case will be able to feel

a tragic end lying in wait for Champlain.

Although the work began with and still belongs to Bogosian, "Talk Radio" in some ways makes for an interesting companion piece to Stone's "Salvador" in its portrait of a driven, self-destructive maverick media figure. Both Champlain and James Woods' journalist in the earlier film bridle at all authority, go too far when restraint might not be in order and seem to will themselves into dangerous situations.

In his attitudes and treatments of all those around him, Champlain is far from sympathetic or likable, but Bogosian commands attention in a patented tour-de-force. At times hard to take because he's clearly in love with the sound of his own voice, he has an undeniable inner demon that compels him ever forward, and Bogosian is utterly convincing as he takes on the world.

Supporting performances are all vividly realized, notably Greene's understanding, all-too-human spouse, John C. McGinley's ever-faithful engineer, Alec Baldwin's harried station manager, Leslie Hope's strained assistant/girlfriend and, in a scene-stealing turn, Michael Wincott's drug-crazed Champlain fan invited to the studio for a tête-à-tête with the host.

Abetted once again by ever-inventive lenser [cameraman] Robert Richardson, Stone has created a beautifully fluid, visually stimulating film out of what started as a 1-set piece. Keyed around Stewart Copeland's score as well as some pop tunes, soundtrack is sharp and the sound mix is very creatively multilayered.   *Cart*

BORN ON THE FOURTH OF JULY

December 20, 1989

Hollywood. A Universal Pictures release of an A. Kitman Ho and Ixtlan production. Produced by Ho, Oliver Stone. Directed by Stone. Screenplay, Stone, Ron Kovic, based on the book by Kovic; camera (Deluxe color), Robert Richardson; editor, David Brenner; co-editor, Joe Hutshing; music, John Williams; sound (Dolby), Todd A. Maitland; production design, Bruno Rubeo; art direction, Victor Kempster, Richard L. Johnson; set decoration, Derek R. Hill; costume design, Judy Ruskin; assistant directors, Joseph Reidy, Stephen J. Lim, David Sardi, Donald J. Lee Jr.; associate producers, Clayton Townsend, Reidy; casting, Risa Bramon, Billy Hopkins. Reviewed at Alfred Hitchcock Theater, Universal Studios, Hollywood, Dec. 14, 1989. MPAA Rating: R. Running time: 144 mins.

Ron Kovic	Tom Cruise
Mr. Kovic	Raymond J. Barry
Mrs. Kovic	Caroline Kava
Donna	Kyra Sedgwick
Charlie	Willem Dafoe
Young Ron	Bryan Larkin
Steve Boyer	Jerry Levine
Tommy Kovic	Josh Evans
Jimmy Kovic	Jamie Talisman
Susanne Kovic	Anne Bobby
Timmy	Frank Whaley
Marine major	John Getz
Lieutenant	David Warshofsky
Marvin	Corkey Ford
Willie	Rocky Carroll
Maria Elena	Cordelia Gonzalez
Mr. Wilson	Tony Frank
Mrs. Wilson	Jayne Haynes

Oliver Stone again has shown America to itself in a way it won't forget. His collaboration with Vietnam veteran Ron Kovic to depict Kovic's odyssey from teenage true believer to wheelchair-bound soldier in a very different war results in the most gripping, devastating, telling and understanding film about the Vietnam era ever.

Pic will be a mightly contender for the best picture Oscar, as well as best actor (Tom Cruise as Kovic), best director and a platoon of others. Box offices both here and abroad will be hosting a very long parade.

Stone, who coproduced, directed and wrote the script with Kovic, creates a portrait of a fiercely pure-hearted boy who loved his country and believed that to serve it and to be a man was to fight a war. It turned out to be Vietnam, and that's where the belief was shattered.

Shooting from very much inside this intense young man's perceptions, Stone creates an often surreal vision of an all-American smalltown Catholic upbringing in which the forces shaping Kovic's values and goals are about as gentle as a blast furnace forging steel.

Way before his hero sees action, Stone shoots this like a war film, with nearly every early scene infused with desperate intensity. From boys playing war in the woods to a Fourth of July parade to a wrestling match, the camera races or slows or sweeps around in circles, until the picture becomes a rollercoaster of feeling.

Even with little dialog, Stone piles up images and sound to make the audience aware of what drives a young man who is packing for the Marines the night his classmates are dancing at the prom.

In 'Nam, things go terribly wrong – young Sgt. Kovic accidentally kills a fellow Marine in battle. His attempted confession is harshly denied him by a c.o. Later, he's shot in the foot, gets up for a gritty round of Sgt. Rock grandstanding, and is hit again and paralyzed.

Typically, Stone drenches the picture in visceral reality, from the agonizing chaos of a field hospital to the dead stalemate of a Bronx veteran's hospital infested with rats, drugs and the humiliation of lying helplessly in one's own excrement.

The U.S. Kovic left behind is unrecognizable, yet as he struggles uselessly to regain control of his body he remains steadfast in his ideas, shouting "Love it or leave it!" at his peacenik brother (Josh Evans).

Sprawling picture unveils one incredible scene after another, from a night when a drunk and unbearably pained Kovic wakes the entire neighborhood shouting about the lies he fell for, to the film's horrifying and comedic emotional nadir, a scene in which two drunken, crazed, wheelchair-bound vets (Cruise and Willem Dafoe), stranded on the roadside in the midst of a desert in Mexico, vent their rage on each other.

Until his turnaround, Kovic's life becomes one long surrealistic nightmare from which there is no escape, not even in Mexico. Film's enormous achievement is that it finds a coherent, dramatically beautiful way to tell this story, so that Kovic does become a soldier and does find his war.

Pic's latter scenes at the political conventions where Kovic's activism takes hold also are stunning in that they bring the story powerfully into the present. Watching the protesters forcibly evicted from the gatherings of establishment and vested interests, with John Williams' moving score rising behind the action, it becomes clear Stone is not telling this story to evoke nostalgia.

Cruise, who takes Kovic from clean-cut eager teen to impassioned long-haired activist, is stunning.

Pic comes from a place so deep inside the character's wounded heart that it is almost unbearable.

Dafoe, as a disabled vet hiding out in a Mexican beach town in a haze of mescal, whores and poker, gives a startling, razor-sharp performance.

Also notable are Caroline Kava as Kovic's religious mother and Frank Whaley as a fellow hometown vet.

Tech credits are all superb, particularly the sound-related work; film gains significant energy and dimension from its complex audio tracks.

Cinematographer Robert Richardson and production designer Bruno Rubeo, both longtime Stone collaborators ("Platoon," "Salvador," "Talk Radio"), make firstrate contributions. That Rubeo's 1950 Massapequa, N.Y., was created near Dallas, where "Talk Radio" was shot, is a circumstance few filmgoers will notice. All design and costume elements re-create the '60s in fascinating authenticity.

"What happened?" cries a veteran in this picture, raising the central question of the Vietnam era. Stone's "Born On The Fourth Of July" is perhaps the most relevant answer yet.

Daws

THE DOORS

March 4, 1991

A Tri-Star release from Carolco of a Mario Kassar presentation of a Sasha Harari/ Bill Graham Films/Imagine Entertainment production. Produced by Graham, Harari, A. Kitman Ho. Executive producers, Kassar, Nicholas Clainos, Brian Grazer. Directed by Oliver Stone. Screenplay, J. Randal Johnson, Stone; camera (Deluxe color, Panavision), Robert Richardson; editor, David Brenner, Joe Hutshing; executive music producer, Budd Carr; music producer, Paul A. Rothchild; sound (Dolby), Tod A. Maitland; production design, Barbara Ling; art direction, Larry Fulton; set design, Steve Arnold, Lisette Thomas; set decoration, Cricket Rowland; costume design, Marlene Stewart; special visual effects, Industrial Light & Magic; visual effects supervisor, Michael Owens; associate producers, Clayton Townsend, Joseph Reidy; assistant director, Reidy; 2nd unit camera, Tom Sigel, Toby Phillips; casting, Risa Bramon, Billy Hopkins. Reviewed at Todd-AO Screening Room, N.Y., Feb. 14, 1991. MPAA Rating: R. Running time: 141 mins.

Jim Morrison	Val Kilmer
Pamela Courson	Meg Ryan
John Densmore	Kevin Dillon
Ray Manzarek	Kyle MacLachlan
Robby Krieger	Frank Whaley
Tom Baker	Michael Madsen
Patricia Kennealy	Kathleen Quinlan
Paul Rothchild	Michael Wincott
Dog	Dennis Burkley
Bill Siddons	Josh Evans
Warhol p.r.	Paul Williams
Nico	Kristina Fulton
Andy Warhol	Crispin Glover
Also with: Billy Idol, Charlie Spradling	

"The Doors" is another trip into 1960s hell from Oliver Stone. This long-awaited look at Jim Morrison's short, wild ride through a rock idol life is everything one expects from the filmmaker – intense, over-blown, riveting, humorless, evocative, self-important and impossible to ignore.

The hype machine has been working overtime to stir up fresh interest in Morrison, one of the psychedelic era's legendary casualties. Initial curiosity should be strong, but spending $40 million on such a venture stands as a heavy risk.

His charisma, look and talent notwithstanding, Morrison was, by all accounts, a real handful, and Stone, despite his professed hero worship, has bluntly presented him as very hard to take.

As rendered with considerable physical accuracy by Val Kilmer, Morrison is drunk and/or stoned practically from beginning to end, providing an acute case study of ruinous excess.

Except for some naive hippie-era euphoria early on, the period of the Doors' preeminence feels like a major bummer filled with bad drugs, bad sex, bad parties and horrible things happening in the world.

Stone rightly makes the times a major part of the tale, for, if Morrison had lived at any other moment, this would have been just a sad story of another drunken Irish poet in love with the notion of his own doom.

The singer's obsession with death and mysticism is rooted, via a sepia-tinged prolog, in a childhood experience in which he views the aftermath of a traffic accident involving some Indians. A tribesman sporadically appears to Morrison thereafter, as if beckoning him to "break on through to the other side."

Action proper begins in 1965, as Morrison the would-be poet and pretentious UCLA student filmmaker hooks up with flower child Pamela Courson (Meg Ryan) and launches a band in Venice with John Densmore, Ray Manzarek and Robby Krieger.

Within six months, the Doors, named after Aldous Huxley's "The Doors Of Perception" courtesy of William Blake, are creating a stir on the Sunset Strip.

Stone and co-scenarist J. Randal Johnson show the Doors being signed by Elektra immediately after getting kicked out of the Whisky a Go Go; their travels to San Francisco for the Summer of Love and to New York where they brush up against the Andy Warhol crowd; and recording sessions that become increasingly difficult because of the lead singer's unhinged state.

Outside of Morrison's abusive, drug-drenched relationship with Courson, only two of his innumerable sexual trysts are detailed – one with the exotic Velvet Underground star Nico, the other with the demonic Patricia Kennealy (Kathleen Quinlan).

In a picture loaded with extended concert sequences, two stand out. After an intense encounter with Kennealy in a bathroom, Morrison is forcibly removed from a New Haven stage for obscenity in 1968. A year later, the bloated crooner creates his debacle in Miami, stumbling recklessly through an appearance before famously exposing himself and being dragged into court.

It all ends a mere two years later in Paris, where Morrison has gone to put the Doors behind him and be a poet. Dead at 27, he joined the many other celebrated artists buried at Père-Lachaise.

Despite his relentless irresponsibility and boorishness, Morrison remains an intriguing figure over the course of the film's long running time. Stone's attitude toward him is problematic, however.

The muckraking journalist in Stone feels compelled to expose the singer's appalling behavior and deficient character. The artist in Stone, however, celebrates Morrison's taboo-breaking and defiance of authority.

Pic suffers from Stone's penchant for pounding away at his points when subtlety and understatement would be welcome. Relationship between Morrison and Courson also is delineated poorly; she seems willing to take anything he dishes out, but why they stick together throughout six years and many other women is a mystery.

Kilmer is convincing in the lead role, although he never allows the viewer to share any emotions. Morrison's own vocals have been skillfully augmented by Kilmer in some sequences.

The usually engaging Ryan brings little to a vaguely conceived part, whereas Quinlan commands the screen.

Much fun has been had with the casting of some incidental roles. Crispin Glover appears as a suitably weird Andy Warhol; co-producer Bill Graham as the New Haven concert promoter; Mimi Rogers as a photographer; Kelly Leach as a "birthday girl"; William Kunstler as Morrison's Miami attorney; Sean Stone, the director's son, as the young Morrison; and Stone himself uncredited, as a UCLA film prof.

"The Doors" succeeds in conveying some idea of what made Jim Morrison a compelling personality, but it also creates the impression that the late 1960s were an awful time to be alive and young.

Cart

JFK

December 16, 1991

A Warner Bros. release presented in association with Le Studio Canal Plus, Regency Enterprises & Alcor Films of an Ixtlan Corp. & A. Kitman Ho production. Produced by Ho, Oliver Stone. Executive producer, Arnon Milchan. Co-producer, Clayton Townsend. Directed by Stone. Screenplay, Stone, Zachary Sklar, based on the books "On the Trail Of The Assassins" by Jim Garrison and "Crossfire: The Plot That Killed Kennedy" by Jim Marrs. Camera (Duart color; Technicolor prints; Panavision widescreen), Robert Richardson; editors, Joe Hutshing, Pietro Scalia; additional editor, Hank Corwin; music, John Williams; production design, Victor Kempster; art direction, Derek R. Hill, Alan R. Tomkins; set design, Mary Finn; set decoration, Crispian Sallis; costume design, Marlene Stewart; sound (Dolby), Tod A. Maitland; associate producer-assistant director, Joseph Reidy; casting, Risa Bramon Garcia, Billy Hopkins, Heidi Levitt. Reviewed at Skywalker Sound, Santa Monica, Calif., Dec. 12, 1991. MPAA Rating: R. Running time: 189 mins.

Jim Garrison	Kevin Costner
Liz Garrison	Sissy Spacek
David Ferrie	Joe Pesci
Clay Shaw	Tommy Lee Jones
Lee Harvey Oswald	Gary Oldman
Lou Ivon	Jay O. Sanders
Bill Broussard	Michael Rooker
Susie Cox	Laurie Metcalf
Al Oser	Gary Grubbs
Dean Andrews	John Candy
Jack Martin	Jack Lemmon
Sen. Russell Long	Walter Matthau
Guy Bannister	Ed Asner
Colonel X	Donald Sutherland
Willie O'Keefe	Kevin Bacon
Jack Ruby	Brian Doyle-Murray
Rose Cheramie	Sally Kirkland
Marina Oswald	Beata Pozniak
Bill Newman	Vincent D'Onofrio
Carlos Bringuier	Tony Plana
Leopoldo	Tomas Milian
Earl Warren	Jim Garrison

A rebuke to official history and a challenge to continue investigating the crime of the century, Oliver Stone's "JFK" is electric muckraking filmmaking. This massive, never-boring political thriller, which most closely resembles Costa-Gavras' "Z" in style and impact, lays out just about every shred of evidence yet uncovered for the conspiracy theory surrounding the assassination of President John F. Kennedy. Pic's contentious P.O.V. [point of view] and agitated manner will stimulate an enormous amount of thought and fresh debate, as well as printed opinion pro and con, assuring the release a high profile even beyond that guaranteed by the Stone and Kevin Costner names.

With a recent Gallup poll indicating that 73% of Americans believe Lee Harvey Oswald did not act alone in killing Kennedy, Stone is apparently playing to an already converted audience that should readily lap up his dramatically presented documentation.

The Warren Report is treated as a cover-up, a myth against which the director, for lack of hard answers that never may be provided, is proposing a myth of his own.

Working in a complex, jumbled style that mixes widescreen, archival footage, tv clips, black & white, slow motion, docu-drama recreations, time jumps, repeated actions from various viewpoints, still photos, the Zapruder film and any other technique at hand, Stone uses the sum of conspiracy theory points made by New Orleans Dist. Atty. Jim Garrison and others since to suggest as strongly as possible that Oswald was, as he claimed before he was killed, "a patsy."

Film will be attacked by establishment mouthpieces and others for its lack of balance, and Stone's customary zeal, crushed idealism and sense of personal betrayal by the government undoubtedly get the better of him here and there. But even if he barks up the wrong tree at times, few films have the advantage of such a fascinating subject, or provoke so many potent questions.

Collaborating on the jam-packed script with journalist Zachary Sklar, Stone launches his epic with President Eisenhower's farewell warning about the dangers of the military industrial complex, then zips through a six-minute docu recap of the Kennedy era.

Arriving at Nov. 22, 1963, action cuts to New Orleans, where Stone introduces Southerners who had reasons to resent or hate the young, liberal president.

Suspicious about aspects of Oswald's former residency in New Orleans, D.A. Garrison (Costner) begins delving into a mysterious netherworld of right-wing, anti-Castro homosexuals populated by the bewigged David Ferrie (Joe Presci), suave businessman Clay Shaw (Tommy Lee Jones) and unpredictable hustler Willie O'Keefe (Kevin Bacon).

With the spectre of Vietnam in the background and the Warren Report putting the official seal on the lone assassin theory, Garrison persists. Numerous witnesses to curious aspects of the killing have died, tremendous inconsistencies crop up, strange ties emerge, and Garrison begins to suspect that the U.S. government's military industrial complex initiated the killing.

This all sounds more like the stuff of documentaries, and "JFK" trades more freely in the techniques of nonfiction

filmmaking than just about any feature this side of "The Battle of Algiers."

In fact, Stone's mixing of styles, designed to promote doubts and alternatives as well as to clarify, stands as an apt visual correlative to the confusion and mystery inherent in the material.

Where Stone takes this beyond documentary, however, is in the film's fabulously rich parade of personalities. With superior character actors and a handful of stars enacting key secondary figures, the picture is an amazing collection of types, from high government and military officials to criminals and lowlifes. Scene after scene is brought vividly to life by first-rate performances that sock over the script's many points.

Starting at the top, Stone uses Costner's Garrison as a sort of Capraesque Everyman, a determined, sometimes misguided, but essentially fair-minded fellow who just wants to get at the truth. Costner may not resemble the real Garrison much, and Stone no doubt slides over many of the attorney's flaws. But the actor, in a low-key but forceful performance, nicely conveys the requisite grit, curiosity and fearlessness.

Particularly noteworthy in the huge cast are Pesci as the volatile Ferrie, Jones as the superbly smooth Shaw, Laurie Metcalf as Garrison's assistant D.A., Gary Oldman as the creepy and offbalance Oswald, Donald Sutherland in a hypnotic turn as the investigator's Deep Throat, Bacon as a trick of Shaw's who squeals, Brian Doyle-Murray as the crude Jack Ruby, a surprising John Candy as a hip adversary of the D.A., Jack Lemmon as an informant, Ed Asner as a former FBI thug, and Michael Rooker and Jay O. Sanders as top assistants to Garrison.

Most conspicuous weakness comes in the depiction of Garrison's home life and in the idealization of Kennedy himself. As the investigator's wife, Sissy Spacek is stuck with almost nothing but nagging lines, complaining that his obsessive quest is driving them apart. Domestic scenes are conventionally portrayed and quickly forgotten once the political momentum picks up again.

It remains a matter of debate as to what Kennedy would have done about Southeast Asia had he lived, as well as how committed he was to civil rights and other liberal issues. The film insists that JFK had already decided to pull out of Vietnam if he won a second term, fully embraced the cause of blacks, wanted to backtrack on nuclear weapons and end the Cold War. Stone suggests these issues brought him to fatal odds with the entrenched powers in Washington, notably the Pentagon, CIA and J. Edgar Hoover, all of whom allegedly saw in LBJ someone they knew would play ball.

All these notions have been batted around for years, but what gives "JFK" so much impact is that they are collected here in one place and assembled so dramatically. Aspects of the case will undoubtedly be argued into eternity, and Stone enthusiastically stokes the fires of the debate.

Pic is filled with consummate technical achievements. Robert Richardson's cinematography further refines the docu-based style he and Stone initiated on "Salvador" and have pursued ever since, with exciting results. Editors Joe Hutshing and Pietro Scalia organized mountains of footage and information from many sources, and made it all work.

John Williams' score is atypical and properly troubling, while contributions of production designer Victor Kempster and his team, as well as costume designer Marlene Stewart, add to the time and place. Many of the actual locations in Dallas, including Dealey Plaza and the Texas School Book Depository, were used to tremendous effect.

Todd McCarthy

HEAVEN AND EARTH

December 27, 1993

A Warner Bros. release presented in association with Regency Enterprises/Le Studio Canal Plus/Alcor Films of an Ixtlan/New Regency/Todd-AO/TAE production. Produced by Oliver Stone, Arnon Milchan, Robert Kline, A. Kitman Ho. Executive producer, Mario Kassar. Co-producer, Clayton Townsend. Directed, written by Stone, based on the books "When Heaven and Earth Changed Places," by Le Ly Hayslip with Jay Wurts, and "Child of War, Woman of Peace," by Le Ly Hayslip with James Hayslip. Camera (Technicolor; Panavision widescreen), Robert Richardson; editors, David Brenner, Sally Menke; music, Kitaro; production design, Victor Kempster; supervising art director (Thailand), Alan R. Tomkins; art direction, Stephen Spence, Leslie Tomkins, Chaiyan (Lek) Chunsuttiwat (Thailand), Woods Mackintosh (L.A.); set design, Jack G. Taylor Jr. (L.A.); set decoration, Ted Glass (Thailand), Merideth Boswell (L.A.); cos-tume design, Ha Nguyen; sound (Dolby), Bill Daly; associate producers, Risa Bramon Garcia, Christina Rodgers, Richard Rutowski; assistant directors, Herb Gains, Sompol Sungkawess (Thailand); second unit camera, Philip C. Pfeiffer; casting, Garcia, Billy Hopkins, Heidi Levitt. Reviewed at Skywalker Sound, Santa Monica, Nov. 19, 1993. MPAA Rating: R. Running time: 140 mins.

Sgt. Steve Butler	Tommy Lee Jones
Mama	Joan Chen
Papa	Haing S. Ngor
Le Ly	Hiep Thi Le
Eugenia	Debbie Reynolds
Sau	Dustin Nguyen
Bernice	Conchata Ferrell
Madame Lien	Vivian Wu
Larry	Dale Dye

With: Liem Whatley, Robert Burke, Michael Paul Chan, Timothy Carhart, Tim Guinee, Catherine Ai.

The U.S. stayed in Vietnam too long, and Oliver Stone has returned to the subject one time too many with "Heaven and Earth." Final installment in the director's trilogy of films on the nation's convulsive recent history represents an attempt to show the war and its aftermath from a Vietnamese POV [point of view], but the sledgehammer approach to storytelling merely results in audience numbness and distance from the potentially moving material. Critical and commercial response will be muted.

This is also Stone's first film centering upon a female protagonist, but, unlike his first two powerful Nam sagas, "Platoon" and "Born on the Fourth of July," this one won't win him any Oscars. Drawing upon two autobiographical works by his central figure, Stone presents nearly 40 years in the life of Le Ly as a succession of events with a melodrama quotient that might have challenged even Joan Crawford or Lana Turner.

The vessel for Stone's latest agitated history lesson is a Vietnamese Buddhist peasant who, in the way she is soiled, dominated, exploited, raped, brutalized, colonized, transformed and torn apart from her family, is no doubt supposed to represent Vietnam itself. Unfortunately, the analogy works better than the personal, emotional story that, even if true down to the smallest detail, as related here comes off as conventional and cliched.

An early-1950s prologue presents the rice-farming community of Ky La, in central Vietnam, as a simple paradise, "the most beautiful village in the world," and indeed it looks to be, a patch of green situated gloriously amid towering limestone peaks. But the French destroyed the quiet hamlet, and subsequently, per the heroine, "everything changed forever" with the arrival of the Viet Cong in 1963.

Le Ly (Hiep Thi Le) sees her two brothers run off to join the Communists, who eventually torture and rape her. To escape the turmoil in the midlands, she flees to Saigon at 18, where she joins a wealthy household but promptly becomes pregnant by the master.

Kicked out of the house but supported financially, Le Ly moves to Da Nang, where her sister has become a cheap whore, then back to her village, where her parents are in dire straits and she's perceived as a tramp.

Back in Saigon, she meets Yank Sgt. Steve Butler (Tommy Lee Jones), who just needs someone to talk to but, of course, is interested in something else from Le Ly as well. He proposes immediately, vowing to take her away from all this and settle her down in San Diego, but it takes three years, and the final evacuation of Americans from the country, for his promise to come true.

At the 90-minute mark, Butler, Le Ly, their son and her previous son arrive in suburbia, and perhaps the film's most effective moments catalogue her experiences seeing American middle-class lifestyles and consumerism for the first time. Butler's family and home are lightly and amusingly caricatured, just enough to let Americans see how others might see them and to create an alien feeling that would take some getting used to.

But over time, which sees the birth of another son, things go better for Le Ly than for Butler, the latter a classic case of a soldier who's kept his wartime atrocities bottled up and cracks under the pressure of a normal life. While his wife slowly works her way up the professional and economic ladder, and finds sustenance in Buddhism, he implodes, resulting in irrational and emotional acts of violence that doom the family as a unit.

Finale, which has Le Ly making her first visit to her native village in many years, provides a way to say that if the U.S. suffered a great deal because of the traumatic war, Vietnam suffered much more and is still suffering.

All this plays just about as melodramatically and simplistically as it sounds, but there are numerous other problems as well. Lecturing tone is set from the beginning, and the accents of the Asian performers, some thicker than others, are not only intermittently hard to wade through, but result in their characters speaking a sort of pidgin English that makes them seem more simple and less natural than they should.

Worst of all is the score by Japanese composer Kitaro, which thunderously announces and then underlines the film's every occurrence. It's almost a parody of a self-importantly dramatic soundtrack, and its incessant insistence upon communicating the picture's import allows for no moments of quiet insight or intimacy.

In writing this screenplay, foreign to him in more ways than one, Stone has taken no overt political position, and consequently adds very little to either the general discussion of Vietnam or his own.

Despite the different perspective, and unlike his two previous pix on the subject, this story doesn't provide him with the forum to say much new or interesting. Nor, despite the intensity of the dramatic situations, does he make it feel personal or impassioned.

Newcomer Hiep Thi Le goes through all the histrionic motions as the beleaguered Le Ly, but the effect of the performance is mostly surface seat and little inner suffering. Jones tries to hit some unusual notes by emphasizing the vulnerable aspects of a professional killer, but that part of the tortured vet never becomes fully dimensional.

Joan Chen is aged and made deliberately ugly to play Le Ly's long-suffering mother in what ultimately seems like serious miscasting. Haing S. Ngor, an Oscar winner for "The Killing Fields," is seen to considerably less effect here as Le Ly's father. Debbie Reynolds has a throwaway in her first screen role in more than 20 years.

Shot mostly in Thailand, with some background views having been grabbed on location in Vietnam, pic looks impressive. Production designer Victor Kempster and his team have done a memorable job recreating the village as well as teeming Saigon, and lenser [cameraman] Robert Richardson has once again fashioned some colorfully dense widescreen images of the recent past.

But the net effect is that Stone and his audience have been here before, and that the point of diminishing returns has definitely been reached.

Todd McCarthy

NATURAL BORN KILLERS

August 15–21, 1994

Stone's 'Killers' A Bloody Good Show

A Warner Bros. release presented in association with Regency Enterprises and Alcor Films of an Ixtlan/New Regency production in association with J D Prods. Produced by Jane Hamsher, Don Murphy, Clayton Townsend. Executive producers, Arnon Milchan, Tom Mount. Co-producer, Rand Vossler. Directed by Oliver Stone. Screenplay, David Veloz, Richard Rutowski, Stone, story by Quentin Tarantino. Camera (Technicolor), Robert Richardson; editors, Hank Corwin, Brian Berdan; executive music producer, Budd Carr; production design, Victor Kempster; supervising art director, Alan R. Tomkins; art direction, Margery Zweizig; set design, John Perry Goldsmith, Stella Furner; set decoration, Merideth Boswell; costume design, Richard Hornung; sound (Dolby), David Macmillan; visual effects, Pacific Data Images; animation sequences, Colossal Pictures; animation designer, Mike Smith; associate producers, Risa Bramon Garcia, Rutowski; assistant director, Herb Gains; second unit director, Philip Pfeiffer; casting, Garcia,   Billy Hopkins, Heidi Levitt. Reviewed at Skywalker Sound, Santa Monica, Aug. 5, 1994. MPAA Rating: R. Running time: 119 mins.

Mickey	Woody Harrelson
Mallory	Juliette Lewis
Wayne Gale	Robert Downey Jr.
Dwight McClusky	Tommy Lee Jones
Jack Scagnetti	Tom Sizemore
Mallory's dad	Rodney Dangerfield
Old Indian	Russell Means
Mallory's mom	Edie McClurg
Gas Station Attendant	Balthazar Getty
Duncan Homolka	Joe Grifasi
Mabel	O-Lan Jones

"Natural Born Killers" is a heavy duty acid trip, quite possibly the most hallucinatory and anarchic picture made at a major Hollywood studio in at least 20 years. As a scabrous look at a society that promotes murderers as pop culture icons, as well as a scathing indictment of a mass media establishment that caters to and profits from such starmaking, the film has a contemporary relevance that no one can miss. It also happens to be Oliver Stone's most exciting work to date strictly from a filmmaking point of view.

Served up in a highly stylized manner, this almost laughably bloody pic will once again stir up the old op-ed [opinion-editorial] page arguments about violence in the cinema that date back to the late '60s. Ensuing controversy will combine with the sheer exhilaration of the piece to provide the marketing upside, while heavy gore quotient will keep many away, resulting in strong B.O. [box office] in certain situations, but something less than widespread appeal.

A rare Stone film in that it's neither historically rooted nor written originally by him, "Natural Born Killers" still shows the bloody fingerprints of its original author, Quentin Tarantino, although Stone has made the material his own (Tarantino receives story credit only) and supplied a thick layer of sociopolitical commentary readily recognizable as his. Using the standby "Gun Crazy"/"Bonnie And Clyde" young-lovers-on-a-killing-spree format but traveling further down that road than anyone has before, the director has made a fiction that might be said to resemble a psychedelic documentary about the American cult of sex, violence and celebrity.

Film is divided into two halves, the first of which vividly, and often outrageously, lays out the crazy three weeks during which the lead couple gun down 52 people out west. The second half presents the insane media circus which surrounds their incarceration, a live in-prison TV interview, a riot and their subsequent amazing escape. The glorification of Bonnie and Clyde that Arthur Penn's film made note of 27 years ago is shown here to have magnified into a virtual definition of a vulgar culture, and seems quite appropriate to an age dominated by such figures as Amy Fisher, the Menendez brothers, Tonya Harding and, yes, O. J. Simpson. Stylistic and thematic motifs are established at once, as some stunningly off-kilter, floating shots, intercut with black-and-white alternates and inserts of animals living and dead, lead up to Mickey (Woody Harrelson) and Mallory (Juliette Lewis) shooting up in a roadside cafe. They kill for the sake of their great love for each other, they say, and the film's psychological ambitions never get much deeper than that. But the wild stylistics will be a turn-on for viewers ready for a visceral ride with the feel of an elaborate souped-up '60s exploitation road picture.

In an audacious comic conceit, flashbacks show Mallory's family life heretofore in literally sitcom terms, as meanie dad (Rodney Dangerfield) bullies and molests her before hunky escaped con Mickey comes along to rescue her and launch their killing spree, a la "Badlands," by knocking off her folks.

As the two leave a trail of blood on New Mexico's infamous Route 66, blowing away people whenever they feel like it, for no reason, but normally leaving one survivor to tell the tale, the killers quickly become the celebs of the moment, in large part due to the spotlighting provided by a show called "American Maniacs," hosted by the fatuous Wayne Gale (Robert Downey Jr.).

After two particularly disturbing episodes, one in which Mallory roughly seduces teenager (Balthazar Getty) before killing him, and another in which Mickey reflexively murders a wise Indian (Russell Means) who has been hospitable to them, the pair are finally cornered by police in Gallup and are taken away.

Their capture, however, merely sends the picture into an even higher gear, as the irrepressible Wayne Gale sets out to capture his highest ratings ever via a live interview with the nation's most prolific killer on Super Bowl Sunday.

At the same time, the unhinged good old boy warden (Tommy Lee Jones) has brought in a tough cop (Tom Sizemore) to quietly eliminate Mickey and Mallory in-house. But during the TV interview, Mickey's survival instincts come to the fore, and he manages to incite a volcanic prison riot that allows the reunited couple to escape, with the hyion, resembling a demonically clever light show at a late '60s rock concert. Picking up technically where he left off on "JFK," Stone, along with his exceptional collaborators, including cinematographer Robert Richardson, editors Hank Corwin and Brian Berdan, production designer Victor Kempster and assorted visual and animation design hands, has served up a dazzling array of images that rivets the attention for two hours.

The narrative is related in color 35mm, black-and-white, Super 8 and video, and at different speeds. As the couple zooms off to some new bloody destination, the backgrounds are shown via blatantly artificial rear projection, while they and their car are bathed in a constantly changing assortment of colored lights. Throughout its course, the film moves from the extremes of stylization, sometimes punctuated by muscular animation inserts, TV recreations, the mock sitcom and film clips (including the Stone-written "Midnight Express" and "Scarface"), to the immediacy of cinema verité and on-the-spot documentary reportage. Everyone and everything is exaggerated and caricatured, but the invention and precision of the style allows it to make its points with impressive clarity. Performers are pushed to the brink, which keeps them entertaining, if uniformly repellent. Harrelson and Lewis are all lust (blood and sex) and no conscience as the pretty couple "naturally born bad." Jones is

broader than he's ever been as the sweaty, lip-smacking warden none too good at his job. Standout perf [performance] comes from Downey, whose imitation of Robin Leach's distinctive cockney accent is hilariously dead-on, and who deftly conveys the true extent to which his character admires his lethal subjects.

A wrap-up montage of celebrity criminals and suspects includes a shot of O.J. Simpson, which merely nails home the timeliness of Stone's dizzying diatribe against a vulture-like media and the irresponsibility of modern culture. Film's style may be akin to a shotgun blast, but it still manages to hit the bull's eye.

Todd McCarthy

NIXON

December 18–31, 1995

'Nixon' loses way in Watergate

A Buena Vista release from Hollywood Pictures of an Andrew G. Vajna presentation of an Illusion Entertainment Group/ Cinergi production. Produced by Clayton Townsend, Oliver Stone, Vajna. Co-producers, Eric Hamburg, Dan Halsted.

Directed by Oliver Stone. Screenplay, Stephen J. Rivele, Christopher Wilkinson, Stone. Camera (Technicolor/B&W, Panavision widescreen), Robert Richardson; editors, Brian Berdan, Hank Corwin; music, John Williams; production design, Victor Kempster; art direction, Donald Woodruff, Richard F. Mays, Margery Zweizig; set design, Henry Alberti, Peter J. Kelly, Charlie Vassar; set decoration, Merideth Boswell, costume design, Richard Hornung; sound (Dolby SR), David Macmillan; associate producer, Richard Rutowski; assistant director, David Sardi; casting, Billy Hopkins, Heidi Levitt, Mary Vernieu. Reviewed at Directors Guild of America Theater, L.A., Dec. 12, 1995. MPAA Rating: R. Running time: 190 mins.

Adding one more panel to his obsessional film portrait of American traumas of the 1960s and early 1970s, Oliver Stone now attempts to put his finger on the self-destructive demons deep within Richard Nixon's character, to decidedly mixed results. Highlighted by numerous strong scenes that go a considerable way toward suggesting the key elements in the 37th president's complex personality, "Nixon" far overstays its welcome with an increasingly tedious final hour devoted largely to slogging through the minutiae of Watergate. Not the lethal broadside many might have expected, pic is inescapably interesting due to the parade of recent history on view, but it finally emerges as an honorable, and rather too strenuous, failure.

Richard M. Nixon	Anthony Hopkins
Pat Nixon	Joan Allen
Alexander Haig	Powers Boothe
E. Howard Hunt	Ed Harris
J. Edgar Hoover	Bob Hoskins
John Mitchell	E.G. Marshall
Ron Ziegler	David Paymer
John Dean	David Hyde Pierce
Henry Kissinger	Paul Sorvino
Hannah Nixon	Mary Steenburgen
John Ehrlichman	J.T. Walsh
H.R. Haldeman	James Woods
Clyde Tolson	Brian Bedford
Charles Colson	Kevin Dunn
Murray Chotiner	Fyvush Finkel
Julie Nixon	Annabeth Gish
Harold Nixon	Tony Goldwyn
'Jack Jones'	Larry Hagman
Nelson Rockefeller	Ed Herrmann
Martha Mitchell	Madeleine Kahn
Herb Klein	Saul Rubinek
Johnny Roselli	Tony Lo Bianco
Richard Nixon at 12	Corey Carrier
Frank Nixon	Tom Bower
Richard Nixon at 19	David Barry Gray
Manolo Sanchez	Tony Plana
Trini Cardoza	Dan Hedaya
Bob	John Cunningham
Earl	John C. McGinley
Gordon Liddy	John Diehl
Frank Sturgis	Robert Beltran
Tricia Nixon	Marley Shelton
Young Student	Joanna Going
President's Lawyer	George Plimpton

Commercial outlook is highly questionable and dependent upon many factors, including how stirred the media and political establishment will feel to debate the film's merits, and how intrigued the public will be, not only by the Nixon name, but by a Stone picture that is uncharacteristically uncontroversial.

Stone and most of his writers have covered most of the bases of Nixon's life – his impoverished religiously strict Quaker upbringing in rural California, his sometimes strained marriage and remoteness as a father, his political ups and downs and amazing central role in several of the key dramas of this century – and do so in a chronologically jumbled manner that lends the proceedings an inelegant shape but endeavors to provide a continual feast of revelations.

Through it all, the filmmakers admirably try to steer the epic yarn in an inward direction, attempting to explain why, as Howart Hunt says, "He's the darkness reaching out for the darkness," or, as Nixon himself crucially asks when Watergate is closing in on him, "Why do they hate me so?"

The answers – a lifelong inferiority complex stemming from his critical father, lackluster academic credentials and homely appearance, the early deaths of his brothers, his impulse to turn political adversaries into personal enemies, his inability to connect with people on an intimate basis – may strike some as amateur Freudianizing, but they would also seem to have more than a bit of truth to them.

In fact, if Stone had stuck with an intense, claustrophobic view of his subject and his closest associates, the picture might have been considerably more powerful, as well as being mercifully shorter. Although "Nixon" more or less holds the attention throughout due to the absorbing history on parade, this is one film in which the viewer feels every one of its 190 minutes.

For starters, pic could have dispensed with the excess of selections from the Oliver Stone stock library of traumatic '60s events; by now, this footage plays like a ritual in a Stone film, so that it takes on the feel of an obligatory high-lights reel.

Beginning with the cause and effect of Watergate, pic slides back in time to Nixon's loss to JFK in the 1960 election – "They stole it fair and square,"one of his advisers quips – and finally back to 1925, with young Dick Nixon in Whittier. Storytelling jumps around willy-nilly in the early going, vaulting ahead to 1962 and Nixon's humiliating loss in the California gubernatorial race and his promise to wife Pat that he'll retire forever from public life.

In one of several nods to "Citizen Kane," an utterly inauthentic mock "March of Time" recounts numerous aspects of Nixon's political career. One of the film's most successful recurring motifs is Nixon's haunted feeling that he climbed to power over the bodies of the dead Kennedys, as well as his lifelong sense that he lived in their shadows.

Looking at JFK's portrait on the wall as he prepares to leave the White House after his resignation, Nixon plaintively says, "When they look at you, they see what they want to be. When they look at me, they see what they are."

On it goes, through Nixon's dubious Cuban criminal connections that led to his links with the Watergate plumbers, his complicity with J. Edgar Hoover and his winning the presidency on the promise of ending the Vietnam War. Weirdly, tale jumps immediately from his victory to the decision to bomb the hell out of Cambodia and the subsequent Kent State massacre.

One of the best scenes shows the president's annoyed but complex reac-tion to the Kent State tragedy while having dinner with his inner circle on his yacht, but this is shortly followed by one of the worst sequences, in which Nixon visits the Lincoln Memorial at 4 a.m. and engages a bunch of hostile students in an awkward discussion.

To Nixon's fury, the mounting details of Watergate come to overwhelm media and public interest in his genuine achieve-ments, and pic's long final act takes its preordained course as all the king's men take the fall while Nixon awaits his fate drinking through the night and listening again and again to his incriminating tapes.

Francois Truffaut once suggested that Ingmar Bergman, the most psychologi-cally oriented of filmmakers, would have been the ideal director for a film of "The Final Days," and there's a touch of such an approach in these later reels.

Unfortunately, there is also far too much Watergate compared with earlier matters that are scarcely mentioned or dramatized, such as what led Nixon into politics in the first place, what shaped his ideology, and his early implementation of dirty tricks despite his moral upbringing. In large measure due to its familiarity, the third hour feels terribly drawn out.

Anthony Hopkins' central performance as Nixon elicits a complicated reaction. In the psychological realm, in locating what he and Stone decided was important in making Nixon tick, in conveying the awareness that his character is a man difficult, if not impossible, to love, he's done an excellent job.

In his consummately actorly way, he convinces the viewer to go along with his rendition of one of modern history's most familiar figures, while adding the vulner-able, personal side that was not often seen. But physically and vocally, he's just not entirely convincing, and one never really forgets that this is an actor giving his best impression of a terribly famous man.

The same could be said for nearly everyone else in the enormous cast, no matter how well they perform. Paul Sorvino, for instance, catches Kissinger's basso voice and phrasings very well, but there is a simultaneous amusement to be had in the stunt of portraying such a distinctive personality. Powers Boothe as Alexander Haig, E.G. Marshall as John Mitchell, Madeleine Kahn as Martha Mitchell, David Hyde Pierce as John Dean and James Woods as H.R. Haldeman are among the most convincing of the impersonations, while Bob Hoskins and Brian Bedford outrageously portray J. Edgar Hoover and Clyde Tolson as a couple of old queens about whom everyone seems to know the truth.

The one performer who cuts deeper is Joan Allen, who gives her Pat Nixon a surprising dimensionality and often touching humanity. This is a public figure no one pretended to understand well,

but Allen provides great insight into a woman who stood by her man through it all, but not without taking him to task for his personal failings and confronting him constantly when he was wrong.

Technically, film is impressive, with some of the White House sets modified from "The American President" and shot in a versatile variety of styles by Robert Richardson. But the mixing of 35mm, video-like images, black-and-white and docu footage, so effective in "JFK" and "Natural Born Killers," seems more arbitrary here and becomes needlessly annoying at times.

Todd McCarthy

Bibliography

The following books and articles were used as background material:

Stone by James Riordan, Aurum, 1996

T*he Cinema of Oliver Stone* by Norman Kagan, Roundhouse Publishing, 1995

Oliver Stone: Wakeup Cinema by Frank Beaver, Twayne Publishers, 1994

'Oliver Stone: A Talk with the Academy Award Winning Screenwriter of Midnight Express About His New Film, *The Hand* – *Mediascene Prevue*, November 1980

'De Laurentis, Stone in Lawsuit' by Michael London – *Los Angeles Times*, 21 December 1984

'Salvador – Drawing a Bead on a Dirty War' – *Los Angeles Times*, 1 December 1985

'Salvador. The Passion of Pulp, the Rush of Ugly Reality', by John Powers – *LA Weekly*, 11 April 1986

'Point Man', by Pat McGilligan – *Film Comment*, February 1987

'Oliver Stone', by Alexander Cockburn – *American Film*, December 1987

'Stone Raids Wall Street', by Peter Biskind – *Premiere*, December 1987

'A Moralist in Movieland', by Paul Rosenfield – *Los Angeles Times*, 20 December 1987

'Oliver Stone', by Marc Cooper – *Playboy*, February 1988

'The Last Exorcism of Oliver Stone' by Elaine Dulka – *Los Angeles Times*, 17 December 1989

'Kovic, Douglas Praise Stone as Filmmaker of Social Change', by Will Tusher – *Variety*, 4 May 1990

'For Oliver Stone, It's Time to Move on from Vietnam', by Glenn Collins – *New York Times*, 2 January 1991

'Stone Unturned', by Mark Rowland – *American Film*, March 1991

'Oliver Stone', by John Powers – *US*, 21 March 1991

'Oliver Stone', by Jeffrey Ressner – *Rolling Stone*, 4 April 1991

'Plunging into the Labyrinth', by Lance Morrow and Martha Smilgis – *Time*, 23 December 1991

'Canceled "Noriega" Project Too Risky, Oliver Stone Says', by Robert W. Welkos – *Los Angeles Times*, 28 May 1994

'The Last Wild Man', by Stephen Schiff – *New Yorker*, 8 August 1994

'Oliver Stone's Natural Born Killers', by Julie Salamon – *Wall Street Journal*, 25 August 1994

'Raw Carnage or Revelation', by David Ansen – *Newsweek*, 29 August 1994

'Welcome to the Jungle', by Francine Russo – *Entertainment Weekly*, 9 September 1994

'Nixon' – *Vanity Fair*, September 1995

'On the Set of Oliver Stone's Nixon' by Holly Millea – *Premiere*, December 1995

'Salvador – Drawing a Bead on a Dirty War' – *Los Angeles Times*, 1 December 1985

'Death of a Salesman', by Richard Corliss – *Time*, 18 December 1995

'Oliver Stone Resumes his Presidential Research', by Bernard Weintraub – *New York Times*, 17 December 1995

'Stone Pic Draws Ire of Nixon Family', by Caroline Lee – *Variety*, 20 December 1995

'The Filmmaker Series: Stone', by Peter Biskind – *Premiere*, January 1996

'Oliver's Twist', by Gregory Cerio – *People*, 22 January 1996